MOVIN' ON

Equipment and Techniques For Winter Hikers

by HARRY ROBERTS

**Stone Wall Press, Inc.
1241 30th St. N.W.
Washington, D.C. 20007**

Distributed by
Stackpole Books
Box 1831
Harrisburg, PA 17105

Published December 1977
Second printing September 1978
Third printing October 1982 — over 15,000 copies in print

Library of Congress Card Number 77-14740
ISBN 0-913276-24-3

CONTENTS

DEDICATION

This book is for Molly, Peggy, Nathaniel and Jared, who accept the fact that a writer in the house is, in the long run, less destructive than red squirrels in the attic.

It's also for the members of the Tennessee Scenic Rivers Association, whose hard work and dedication saved Clear Creek and the Obed River for all of us.

HNR
Rotterdam Junction, N.Y.
October, 1977

INTRODUCTION

A few years ago I wrote a small, hardnosed book about backpacking called *Movin' Out*. It was a basic book; mostly information for the beginner with some ethical considerations about the wilderness stirred in, and frosted with what I called philosophy. Some folks called it "smartass", others "down-to-earth" and "practical." Facing the winter head-on is most serious business, so my critics will be pleased that any "smartass" is gone.

This is the same kind of book—a basic text on winter hiking and backpacking. It assumes some three-season backpacking experience; in fact, it virtually mandates it. Winter's the time to learn about winter, not the time to learn how to start your stove.

If you're a seasoned winter peakbagger already, you'll find that a lot of this is elementary, and you'll find repetitions at times. That's okay. I've found that control of the basics makes advanced techniques simple—and many years as a teacher have convinced me that some things need repeating. You may also disagree with some of my judgements on equipment and techniques. That's fine too. You've survived and flourished with your approach; I have with mine. The injunction to the novice should be clear, then. Very few things are final and absolute about winter hiking and camping. What one person considers an eternal truth, another may consider to be heresy. I've seen rational adults reduced to sputters and blubbers in the course of a discussion about the relative merits of down and synthetics as insulation, and I've refereed one dogfight as editor of *Wilderness Camping* about vapor barriers. I'll try, in the course of this book, to differentiate between those things that work for me, those things that work for most folks, and those things that all winter freaks consider absolutes.

There won't be much tabular data here. It'll seem strange, perhaps, to read a book on winter that doesn't contain a windchill chart, but if you have ever walked to the post office on a windy 15° day, I don't need to tell you that it felt a whole lot colder than 15°! How much colder exactly doesn't really matter, provided you recognize the danger inherent in those three words, "a whole lot". There won't be any weight

1

versus size tables for snowshoes, either. And there won't be any calorie value tables for various foods. There won't be a Beaufort wind scale or a metabolic expenditure chart or even a performance level chart for stoves. Tables are for scientists. Winter hiking is for artists.

We'll be talking mostly about the Northeast for several reasons. The first—and best—is that New York's Adirondacks and New Hampshire's White Mountains represent the sub-arctic world at its best (and worst). The weather is severe; it can change with terrifying suddenness, and it's damp. If you want to train for a winter ascent of McKinley, come to the summit of New Hampshire's Mt. Washington, where the average wind velocity in January is a rousing 50 m.p.h. and you can expect measurable snowfall three days out of five. Not bad—especially when coupled with temperatures that are usually subzero. On one memorable day, April 12, 1934, the summit station recorded a gust of 231 miles per hour.

That's not the kind of winter experience we're going to talk about, though. We're going to be in the relatively sheltered low country for the most part, where the wind is broken by the trees and the surrounding hills. But it'll still be cold up there, at the head of Avalanche Pass. And the Adirondack powder will be deep. And you might, just might, wake up to rain on the next day. If you're comfortable on a Northeast winter hike, you'll survive—yes even flourish—just about anywhere in the world.

We're going to talk about a lot of old-timey approaches to the winter in this book. There were some remarkable cold-weather journeys made on this continent long before down clothing and sleeping bags and gasoline-fired stoves. An ounce of good sense and knowledge is worth many pounds of equipment carried by a fool. There's gear in your closet that you probably never thought of as suitable for winter camping—but it is. There's gear at the Salvation Army and at your local work clothes store, too.

Finally, I'd be remiss if I didn't note that the winter world, like all other real worlds, makes precious few sex distinctions. I prefer real worlds. If I use "he" and "him" at times instead of "he/she", and "him/her" it's to avoid some unlovely gram-matical construction rather than to imply that women have no place outdoors in winter.

Now that we know each other a bit, let's move on—into the winter! □

THE FIRST STEPS

Getting started with winter hiking is the same gradual process you probably went through when you started roaming the trails in summer. Chances are good that you didn't begin with a five-day backbreaker in the toughest, spikiest terrain in three states. Well, I don't recommend beginning your winter experiences with a week in the Bitterroots or a January traverse of the Presidentials, either. I'd recommend a short tramp around nearby familiar terrain on a brisk, clear day in November or December before the snow has fallen—at any rate, before enough has fallen that you need snowshoes.

The first stop is your closet, not your friendly local outfitter's shop. If you're a summer hiker, you have most of what you need already, and what you don't have and may need we'll talk about later. Find your daypack, your little daytripping buddy, put it on the floor, and we'll start to throw things at it. First your hiking boots, which were sized (you'll remember) to fit over two pairs of socks, one heavy and one light. They'll do for now. If they haven't been waterproofed lately with Sno Seal, make a note to do it. Wool socks, of course—unless you're allergic to wool, in which case you'll want Orlon socks next to your hide.

Next comes an old pair of pants. Wool pants, although I'll settle for Orlon whipcord. If you're a guy, chances are good that there's an elderly suit hanging in there that's dramatically out of fashion. Those baggy, rumpsprung pants will be just dandy. In time, you'll make some alterations to them. You'll let out the cuffs because you don't want cuffs in winter any more than you do in summer. In fact, even less. You need two cuffsful of wet snow like a bullsnake needs a baseball bat! In fact, you can let down the cuffs, turn the legs up to a height that won't catch your heel, and hem them there after cutting off the excess fabric while your boots are drinking their fill of Sno Seal tonight. You don't need a sewing machine for this operation; in fact, it's easier for me to nail down the hem by hand. Bear in mind, however, that I once ran a sewing machine needle through my thumb, thread and all, and when asked incredulously how it had happened, proceeded to recreate the situation *in toto*, thread and all! Hint: when you

3

get the fabric turned up inside where you want it, pin it in place with some straight pins, and press it so it stays put.

Regretably, the dictates of fashion make it unlikely that most women have immediate access to reasonably loose woolen pants. Jeans, maybe; wool, rarely. Jeans are a no-no for cold weather hiking. To enlarge on that dictum, cotton is a no-no. We'll talk about why later. For the time being, take my word for it.

No honest tightly-woven woolen pants around? Well, off to the outfitter's. Only in this case, the outfitter is the nearest Army-Navy store.

You're looking for mediumweight G.I. (or Air Force) sur-plus woolen pants. The last pair I bought, in 1974 cost me $2.98! If they're in good shape, you may have to go all of seven bucks for them. They're worth it. Get them roomy. The Navy bell-bottomed wools are even warmer, although they're hard to find and rather expensive. No G.I. pants around? Well, head for the Salvation Army or Goodwill store and pick up a stout pair of sharkskins or worsteds for less than five bucks a pair. If you feel more affluent, Johnson Mills, up in the chilly Northeast Kingdom part of Vermont makes great dark green woolen pants—heavy woolen pants—for not too much money (under $20 last year). They're a Northeast phenomenon. Look for them in general stores in rural areas or in city stores that specialize in work clothes. If there's a shop like that in town, you'll learn to love it. They have good, unfancy wool shirts at a fair price (usually Melton or Johnson in the Northeast), good unlined leather mittens ("chopper mitts") at good prices, and other very functional goodies for folks who work in the cold at prices that make the shopping mall joints look like true ripoffs.

While we're on the topic of wool pants, Woolrich makes fine ones (particularly the Malone pants) and Filson, a Seattle outfit, makes pants out of a light, hard-finish wool called *"cruiser cloth"* that are too good to be true. You don't find that kind of fabric every day.

Okay. The boots are proofed, the woolen pants are ready. Somewhere in some closet there has to be a short-sleeved polyester shirt that looks like a fishnet. They were a fashion item up until a year ago, so most folks have one or more around. It's a great undershirt in cold weather.

4

The polyester doesn't sop up water like cotton does; the holes permit lots of air circulation to keep your clothing dry when you've worked up a head of steam, and provide a neat device for trapping still, warm air when you button up. Don't have one? Use a polyester sport shirt or blouse as an undershirt. Don't use a cotton T-shirt. **Cotton kills.** Not on the clear, calm day you'll go out in, surely, but later—who knows?

Over this goes a wool shirt, preferably a little oversized and with flaps over the pockets. I commend your local work clothing shop to your attention for this if you don't have one. Or go to your outfitters and get a Woolrich in salt-and-pepper pattern, the old diagonal Ballard Malone weave that wears like iron. For the time being, though, a woolen or Orlon sweater (one heavy or two light) will do nicely.

Over that goes a parka. For the time being, a good single nylon shell that covers your butt and has a hood that protects your face will do nicely. In time, you'll want a real mountain parka if you really get into winter. We'll talk about that later.

Next comes a woolen hat. Yeah, I'll settle for Orlon. It should be big enough to keep your ears warm, and it's a vital piece of gear. If you're ever faced with a choice of carrying an extra hat or an extra pair of mittens, opt for the hat. You can contrive a method to protect your hands. Socks, for example, make admirable mittens. Handwarmer pockets *do* work. Armpits are always available. But you lose such an enormous amount of heat through your scalp that the loss of a hat can literally kill you when the going gets tough.

Next comes mittens. We'll examine a lot of options later on, but for the time being, wool mittens with an unlined leather shell to slip over them are what to look for. For this short trip you could dispense with the shell. You'll need it later, but not now.

Throw your poncho or rain gear in the pile, and you're all suited up. With a few additions, you're set for day trips in quite cold weather with this gear. And there it was, masquerading as everyday clothing in your closet!

When you leave for that two or three hour jaunt around a nearby reforestation area, take your sunglasses if there's even a light dusting of snow on the ground. And give yourself a treat. Take along a vacuum bottle of hot tea or coffee. You can afford the weight on *this* trip.

You liked it! There's no people, either. The leaves are off the trees, permitting wide-ranging views, and the air has a smack and tang to it that you can almost taste with each breath. The other season that most folks hide from seemed like a real treat. Good. Welcome to the club. Now it's time to look into the winter world in depth! □

COLD — HOW IT AFFECTS YOU

The human being is apparently a remarkably adaptable organism. He survives and even thrives over an incredible range of temperature. On closer examination, the vaunted adaptability of the human is largely learned. It's a product of acclimatization and suitable clothing selection.

When I was a kid, cars didn't come with heaters as standard equipment. Heaters were a costly option, and my father didn't have one in a car until 1949. He was afraid that a heated car would make him "dozy." This doesn't mean sleepy or drowsy; it means rotten, specifically with regard to wood. It's a step before "punky," which is, of course, one step before disintegration. My car has a heater, such as it is. (Volkswagen's engineers must have feared making the Herrenvolk dozy too.) But even today, I feel a little guilty when I turn on the heat in the car. That I, that we all, will some day grow dozy, then punky, is inevitable. I just don't always feel right about expediting the process!

My father wasn't an authority on man in a cold environment. He was a farm boy turned house carpenter and, later on, small contractor. He worked outside virtually all his life, and I never saw him wear anything heavier than cotton work gloves. His typical attire was a hat, a pair of Carhart coveralls over a wool cardigan, wool pants, old-fashioned balbriggan underwear or a woolen "union suit," wool socks and felt boots. Granted, the nature of his work rarely kept him outside in winter rain, but it often kept him outside for a full day in temperatures that were well below zero. He was neither more nor less heroic than any worker whose job required that he be outside. He simply spent enough time outdoors in cold weather to become acclimated.

Most folks don't have that option. The bulk of us work in well-heated buildings with little chance to acclimatize. Naturallly we can help the process a bit by keeping our homes at an ecologically responsible temperature and, at the same time, dressing lightly. But mostly we can't depend on a solid, deep-down acclimatization to help us. We will rarely be able to sleep on the snow with only a blanket like the Sherpas. It will help if you're young and in good aerobic condition. It will help if your recreations generally keep you out of doors. But

7

what will enable you to enjoy yourself in winter is solid preparation based on a few physical principles.

You're a heat engine. You may be both wise and beautiful as well, but you're still a heat engine whose core is happiest at 98.6°F. The fuel you burn is food, and in cold weather you'll burn a fair amount of fuel to simply maintain your core temperature—more than half again as much as you would in a more balmy climate. Some of this is unavoidable. No matter what clothing you're wearing, you're still faced with breathing extremely cold air, warming it, and saturating it with water vapor, which can account for as much as 18 percent of your heat loss. Saturation of inspired air represents a steady, predictable 8 or 9 percent loss. Warming the air is a more variable factor. Evaporation of perspiration, another unavoidable loss, accounts for another 18 percent or so. That's 36 percent, give or take a few points, that you can't control. The rest you can control, and how well you control it is the difference between a romping good time and a tragedy!

You can control heat loss by clothing (for which also read "shelter") and by diet. Clothing and shelter can only conserve heat; they can't create it. Only your body can do that, and to do it, it needs food, lots of it. The winter hiker's lunch, it is often said, begins while he's putting away the breakfast gear, and if that's an exaggeration, it's a small one.

What happens if you can't control heat loss? Well, within certain narrow limits, not much. You feel chilly around the edges, that's all. You're not even uncomfortable. If your body temperature drops a little more, about 95°, you shiver, which is the body's way of forcing an isometric contraction and triggering a stored glycogen "dump" from the liver. Below 95°, the shivering becomes uncontrollable. **THIS IS YOUR LAST WARNING!** The onset of uncontrollable shivering indicates that your body is making a last ditch effort to produce heat, and if it fails, what happens thereafter is irreversible without some external heat sources. Write that indelibly in some active pocket of your mind. If uncontrolled shivering fails to reverse the downward plunge of your temperature, the process thereafter is irreversible without external heat source.

Let's see what happens after that. You should know because somebody's life may hang on your ability to recognize what's happening. If shivering turns things around, the shiverer will probably be fussing loudly about the burning and tingling of his fingers and toes, which are well below 95° because the body has shut down blood flow to them in an effort to conserve heat.

This doesn't mean that everything is perfect, not in the least. But they could be worse. If shivering doesn't work, the body shuts down blood flow even more. The extremities become numbed; in fact the victim (and victim is the word) may mutter something about feeling warmer. He isn't. He's dying—unless you do something. By this time, blood pressure and pulse have dropped dramatically, and the combination of reduced blood flow and a diminished volume of oxygen in the blood make the victim glassy-eyed and incapable of rational action. Movement is clumsy, speech is slurred and reflex action essentially ceases.

At this point, the downhill slide accelerates. The body simply quits. The throttling mechanisms that shut down the flow of blood to the extremities fail, and the already cool blood returns to the limbs to be cooled even more. The victim becomes comatose, and at a core temperature of 75° to 80°, he dies. The final, fatal temperature drop can occur with dramatic speed once core temperature drops below 90°. Don't waste time in treating this situation, because you have no predictable time span in which to operate. Get on it!

But how? Well, if you recognize the problem early, with the first burst of shivering, it may be as simple as resting and putting on dry mittens or a hat. It may require a fast change out of sweat-soaked clothing. It may require some quickly-assimilated food and hot drink. It may require all of the above. Essentially, what we've done here is to cut down further heat loss by adding clothes and removing damp clothes and replacing them with dry clothes, add a little more fuel to the tank by providing food, reduce the energy requirement by resting, and add a little physical heat (and a lot of psychological heat) with a cup of something hot, be it no more than water.

If the victim is past that stage, more heroic measures are needed. In order of priority, reduce further heat losses (shelter, dry clothing, more clothing) and then provide an external heat source (a fire; warm water in canteens placed in the armpits, in the neck close to the carotid artery, on chest and belly; nude warm bodies in a sleeping bag array with the victim in between; warm stones—you name it.) If you're with a party of hikers—and in winter you should be, of which more later—these things would be done simultaneously.

I must note that too rapid a rewarming, which will stimulate a massive return of cooled blood from the extremities, can create a coronary incident. The possibility of this happening in the field is pretty remote, but plopping somebody who's thoroughly chilled into a hot tub or shower is an unacceptable risk.

If this sounds to you like we've been discussing hypothermia, you're right. Why didn't I call it *hypothermia* when I started to talk about it? Simple. Hypothermia is a word that backpackers see so often in print that they shrug, think, "Oh, I know all about *that*," and flip through the section without really seeing the words. If I tricked you, I'm glad— and you might be too, some day.

So—hypothermia exists in winter. It exists in summer also. Don't forget that. And it's more often triggered by a combination of wind, wet and cold than by cold alone. In fact, just plain dry cold, even at bizarre extremes like -30°F, is far more manageable and far more pleasant than +20° with wet snow and rain falling and a harsh wind blowing. I'll take the dry, still 30° below **any day!**

The other noticeable physiological response to cold is, of course, frostbite. Like hypothermia, it is assisted by fatigue, lack of food, dampness, dehydration and lack of awareness of the onset of the problem.

Frostbite, in simple terms, is a burn. It occurs when flesh is exposed to a combination of cold, wind and moisture; or it occurs when one's extermities are subjected to extremely diminished circulation. The former usually results in nothing more serious than a more or less uncomfortable "forst nip" of the cheeks, nose or ears. Your best protection against that is a hat that can be pulled down over the ears and a deep, generously cut wind parka hood. Fingers and toes can get frost-nipped too in the course of a long, hard day, but awareness of that unpleasant initial tingle can go a long way toward obviating the problem. Awareness and dry socks and dry mittens are excellent insurance against it. But wet socks, wet mittens, tight boots, fatigue, hunger, dehydration—these things, which usually come in bunches and which come to the unwary with terrible suddenness, cause the real thing.

Frost-nip—the classic white spot on the cheek or the nose—can be taken care of quickly by application of a warm, dry glove or a warm hand. It'll sting, but cause no more problem than a sunburn. Chilled hands can be coped with by heavier mittens, or by plopping your hands under your armpits. Chilled toes? Jog a bit; wiggle your toes; move about. If they still feel uncomfortably cold, change out your socks, and eat and drink some water or hot tea. Catch it early and it's no problem. Get numbed by fatigue and hunger, though, and you don't catch it early, when there's that unpleasant tingle to warn you, because you weren't listening to your body. The next stage, true frostbite, sets in. And that's painless, because what happens is that the water in your flesh freezes, blood (and, of course, oxygen) is excluded, the nerve endings go to sleep, and the extremity turns white, stiff and very cold.

Most winter hikers are cold from time to time, particularly their extremities. The keys here are visual checks and a diminished—or vanished—sensation of pain or discomfort.

Once frostbite has been diagnosed, the treatment is to restore circulation by **gradual** thawing of the part. Do not rub or massage the part, please. There's damaged flesh laced through with tiny, sharp crystals of ice under your care. Massage or manipulation will only tear the flesh more. Mild frostbite can be treated by rewarming the affected parts of the victim's body against your warm skin. Let me tell you, anybody who's willing to warm a frostbite victim's feet against his or her bare belly deserves a wreath of laurel. But if you hike in the winter, you'd better be prepared to do it. You may never have to. I've only had to do it on a few occasions. But if it's got to be done and you're there, you'll do it. You'll know that your treatment is working when your friend begins to yell. Frankly, it hurts like hell to have a mild frostbite thawed.

Thawing a mild frostbite may result in blisters. Treat these like burn blisters. Keep them clean and covered. In my opinion, thawing severe, deep frostbite in the field is a chancy situation. It requires either long, gradual warming or, optimally, immersion of the hand or foot in a 105° water bath—not exactly easy to come by on the trail. It's a delicate chore that leaves the victim traumatized and incapacited with deep third-degree burns, in effect. If the affected member is a foot, the injured party must not walk on it. If it's a hand, it must be considered unusable. And the thawed member, in addition to being subject to massive infection, cannot be permitted to freeze again. Unless you can build a snug snow shelter, insure competent field treatment, and plan for a quick evacuation, you're probably ahead of the game to conduct a forced march out and seek *immediate* help at the nearest hospital. You run a risk here that the area of frostbite damage will extend or worsen, but unless you're equipped to do the rewarming right, the risks of doing it wrong are far worse.

Those are the hazards—hypothermia and frostbite. In the beginning stages, they're of little consequence, and if you catch them then—and the signs are easy to see—it's little more than a sharp rap on the knuckles from a tough, uncompromising environment. If you let them go beyond those initial stages, you've gotten into deep trouble—and you're going to have to get out of it yourself. There's no ski patrol out there.

If this scares you a little, it should. I've seen too many people get into bad trouble in several wilderness pursuits—climbing and whitewater paddling being the main ones—because they went into them with no awareness of the hazards and no concept of how to get out of trouble once they were in it. Short day trips around home on well-known trails offer little potential for disaster, and if you start with them and gradually extend your range into long day trips and over-nights before you tackle the big trips, you'll grow in awareness of what your body's trying to tell you and you'll grow in confidence and poise. As I said, the winter is no time to learn how to start a stove. You shouldn't wait until you're caught in a whiteout at Plateau Leanto on Marcy to decide that you'd better know how to read a map or prepare a snow cave shelter. You learn those things on your friendly local tote roads and in your local reforestation areas. Then, when the time comes to do that traverse of the Divide on cross-country skis, you're ready. You know what's out there—and what's inside you, too. And when *that* happens—why, winter just becomes the best season of all! □

INSULATION

I suppose everybody would be happy if I'd simply launch into a chapter on sleeping bags and a chapter on clothing by telling you what I use by brand name so you could dash into your favorite outfitter's and quote me by chapter and verse. I will tell you what I carry—but not now. Right now, I'd like to talk with you about insulation. That's what keeps you warm.

Before we talk about types of insulation and configuration of insulation, let's get a few basics out of the way. No amount of clothing can ever *produce* heat; it can only *conserve* the heat that you produce. If you're not producing enough heat to maintain normal body temperature, you'll be cold regardless of what you're wearing. It may be, of course, that what you're wearing is soaking wet with sweat, or insufficiently protected against wind penetration, but that's another matter. If you're tired, dehydrated and hungry; you'll be cold in winter. Put on dry clothes, put on "warm" clothes, to be sure. Minimize the heat loss with insulation. But at the same time, get your body back to where it's producing heat by eating, drinking, and resting.

There are various ways in which we lose heat. Some of them are essentially uncontrollable; several others—radiation, conduction and convection—we can control with proper insulation and with good judgement. Conductive heat loss is omnipresent as long as your feet are in contact with the snow. Proper boots drastically reduce this loss, but you can make up for the effectiveness of your boots by parking your duff on a cold, snowy log or by grabbing an aluminum ice axe with an ungloved hand or by falling face-first in the snow.

Radiative heat loss cannot occur if your insulation layer is thick enough to maintain your outer layer of clothing (or your sleeping bag) at ambient temperature. At any rate, if you're even close to enough insulation, radiation loss isn't great.

The bugaboo is heat loss by convection, or in simpler terms, by cool air in motion lifting heat from our warm bodies and whisking it away. Fortunately, air that's in close proximity to any surface tends to like to stay there. "Close" in this case means about an eighth of an inch. This means that in absolutely still, dry air, even bare flesh will retain a tiny warm

13

blanket for a little while. There's an elaborate joke involved with this phenomenon, by the way. The winter hiker will tank up on hot tea or cocoa before bedtime to warm his body up and provide fuel for the long night. Needless to say, this usually requires a cold, cold trek to the latrine at some bleak, improbable hour like 3:00. I've always dressed (sort of) for these forays, but some of my hardier friends with degrees in thermodynamics ridicule the effort to dress by saying that if you move slowly enough, you won't disturb that 1/8-inch of warm air. The watchword is, "Don't go turbulent!"

However preposterous the above might seem, the magic 1/8-inch boundary layer of air that clings to an object unless displaced by wind is real, and is the basis of insulation. If 1/8 inch of air is, by definition, still air, then an insulating garment or sleeping bag need only be able to chop air up in still 1/8-inch segments to keep circulating air from transferring our heat away from us. The other lesson to be learned is that, all other things being equal, the value of the insulation is purely a function of the overall thickness of the insulation. In other words, down equals feathers equals steel wool equals newsprint. "All other things being equal" is, of course, the sneaky clause. Some insulators that would maintain that magic 1/8-inch are literally sieves that would permit too much wind penetration. Take a simple instance. If I swathe you in a jacket and pants made of, say, *PolarGuard* continuous filament polyester insulation, and construct that garment of cheesecloth, any vagrant breeze will penetrate the cheesecloth and the insulation layer to a depth that's a function of wind velocity versus insulation density. If I build the same *PolarGuard* garment out of, say, 110 x 140 count nylon taffeta, the wind penetration will be effectively zero. The only effect would be in those areas where the wind compressed the batting to a thinner cross-section, assuming the insulation is thick enough that the outer skin of the garment is at ambient temperature. Too thin an insulation layer, which would result in a garment skin temperature above ambient, will lose heat to any breeze that wanders by in addition to losing heat by radiation.

Certain other factors enter into this discussion. While insulation value is a function of thickness, high humidity can diminish the effectiveness of insulation. Moist air is a more efficient heat transfer medium than dry air. Further, insulation density can be a factor in overall efficiency if the insulation layer is subjected to wind penetration. It's obvious that the denser layer will reduce wind penetration, just as a denser weave of fabric is more wind-resistant than an open weave.

Insulation density is controllable. You can reduce wind losses by wearing a shell garment of a suitably tight weave. Obviously, you can't control atmospheric humidity, any more than you can control another form of evaporative heat loss—breathing. You *can* control your own perspiration to an extent, and it's important that you do, because evaporative heat loss carries away more calories than just the heat of moisture leaving the body. Each gram of sweat that evaporates robs you of the heat it took to raise it to temperature *and* the latest heat of evaporation as well. And where does all that water go to? Hopefully to the air. Realistically, it enters your insulation, raises its humidity (and heat transfer capacity), and robs it of its convective insulation properties. In extreme cases, your garments can become so soaked that the air spaces collapse, and you're effectively wearing a jacket made of water as far as your heat losses are concerned. Cotton is notorious for losing its air spaces when wet; hence the mountaineer's adage, **Cotton Kills.** Down, for all its worth as a light, comfortable, superbly efficient insulator, also collapses when wet. All insulation loses some value when wet, even if it doesn't collapse, because moist (or saturated) air is a better heat transfer medium. In two words— keep dry!

If you can't—and we have to accept the idea that accidents can happen—an English study of wet clothing might be of interest. It might even save your hide someday. The English are a hardy breed, and among the favorite citizen-oriented competitions is the long distance walk. These are typically held in damp, chilly weather—although there isn't much choice most of the time. The walker's attire is light— usually a string shirt, shorts, a very light sweater and a light nylon windshell. Sometimes trousers or sweatpants are worn. Deaths from hypothermia have occurred on these walks when the competitors were sweat- (or rain-) soaked and subjected to high winds at temperatures above freezing.

In a series of experiments undertaken as a result of several deaths in one competition, physiologist L. Pugh measured the insulation value of the typical walker's garb dry (1.8 clo, or 1.8 men's business suits) and wet (0.18 clo) in a windless environment. In other words, the wet clothes had only a tenth of the insulating value of the dry ones! Assuming that wetness in such competitions is inevitable, Pugh then measured the insulating value of the wet clothing when the wearer was protected (after the fact) by a waterproof anorak. The wet clothing then tested 1.0 clo, or an increase of a bit over five times in insulating value. The impermeable waterproof anorak did little if anything to reduce convective heat loss, but it dramatically reduced evaporative heat loss—enough so that it would well spell the difference between mere discomfort and severe physical trauma or even death on the trail.

Most illustrative of this is the wet suit worn by virtually all knowledgeable whitewater paddlers in cold waters for protection against immersion. It's inevitable that the suit will be sweaty within and wet without from spray, and in the course of a few hours, one gets chilly. **Very** chilly. So, some of us who are longer in the tooth and spindlier in the shank, and less fueled by the fires of youth will wear a light, one-layer, coated nylon paddling jacket over the wet-suit. Its value as insulation against convective heat loss is nil—but it dramatically reduces evaporative heat loss. While you're still swimming in your own sweat, you're comfortably warm. Remember, this is a situation in which ventilation isn't feasible, because ventilation would destroy the primary usefulness of the wet suit, which is to protect the wearer against water of a temperature that could kill him in five to seven minutes.

The lesson's clear. In the unlikely event that a hiker should become fully immersed and spare clothing isn't available (although it should be!), the only recourse may be to swathe the soaking wet walker, clothes and all, in waterproof gear like a rain parka and rain pants, and throw a dry parka **over** the rain parka until other measures (like a fire and warm drinks and shelter) can be devised. Stripping the victim would expose already soaking wet flesh to an unacceptably high level of frostbite risk and a totally unacceptable rate of heat loss. In this case, "half clothed" is surely better than unclothed. If the day is relatively mild and it isn't too far to the "outside," a healthy, well-fed hiker could, with a parka over the rain gear, "walk his clothing dry" if it was wool and polyester fiberfill. It's a bummer—but if there are no alternatives, it's better than hypothermia!

The question inevitably arises about any insulation, be it a sleeping bag or a parka, of "how warm is it?". There's no simple answer. The QMC charts, for example, indicate that three inches of insulation is sufficient for a sleeping person to maintain a steady heat state at -20°F, but this is dependent on several factors. It assumes a full three inches on all sides of the sleeper, that the sleeper is at normal body temperature when he or she crawls in the sack, and it assumes neither wind loss nor evaporative loss due to wet or damp insulation. But it is a place to start. These data also note that one inch of insulation will maintain a steady heat state in a walker at -40°F, again assuming no wind loss, a true inch of dry insulation, and a healthy walker. In point of fact, you don't need much insulation to maintain warmth at terribly low temperatures as long as you're dry, protected from the wind, healthy and well-fed, and moving. Let any of those delicately-poised "as long as's" topple, and your insulation requirements soar. A damp inch of insulation, again assuming no wind loss, is marginal at 40° **above.** *Eighty degrees between wet and dry!!* Make a strong mental note!

I'm going to break a rule I established earlier and show you the QMC data in graphic form below. This chart will clearly demonstrate what's **possible.** I'm also going to show you similar data modified to a more realistic base of 27° protection for a sleeper as opposed to the QMC's 40° protection for a sleeper per inch of insulation. Other data has been modified proportionately, in the ratio of 27:40, and radiation effects of radial sections have been neglected.

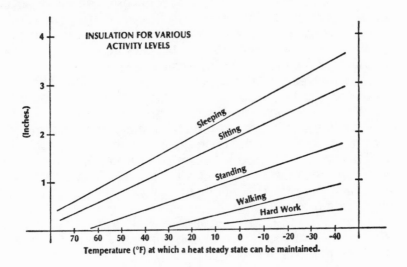

Temperature (°F) at which a heat steady state can be maintained.

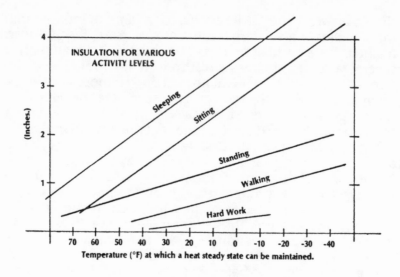

INSULATION FOR VARIOUS ACTIVITY LEVELS

Sleeping
Sitting
Standing
Walking
Hard Work

(Inches.)

70 60 50 40 30 20 10 0 -10 -20 -30 -40

Temperature (°F) at which a heat steady state can be maintained.

This rather more conservative approach can allow us a **little** sweat, or a **little** less insulation under our sleeping bag, or a **little** fatigue. It does not, however, account for crisis situations. Again—a hiker who is not producing enough heat to maintain a steady state with reasonable insulation is a tired, hungry hiker who requires rest, fluids and food. Additional insulation beyond that necessary to maintain ambient temperature at the outer shell of the insulator will do no good at all! Let me amend that. It will do some psychological good, which may have a desirable physiological effect. The tired, hungry, chilly hiker almost always feels like a drag on the party—and some macho winter trippers get their jollies by reinforcing this idea. If you're leading a party, or if you're part of the usual leaderless group of friends off for a day trip or a weekend, I assume you won't engage in that kind of puerile nonsense or let anybody else engage in it. We all get tired. Our bodies aren't totally predictable machines. The important thing is to make the dead tired walker feel comfortable and a part of the group. You're tired, too, I'll bet. Simple acknowledgement of that fact will relax your bushed companion and let him use his heat to warm his body, not to evaporate tension sweat.

Sorry for the aside—but I've seen too many people driven back to the boob tube in winter by their dumbjock trail companions. It seems to be a particularly prevalent corrosive game that men play on their wives or on novices who aren't quite friends—some dude you work with and get along with, but don't really know too well. I could explore the whys of this for a hundred pages, but I won't. Don't do it yourself and don't hike more than once with people who do. I'm a marathon canoe racer and a sometime citizen racer on X-C skis. I know what it's like to be tired; I know how vulnerable we all are. End of sermon. End of digression.

Back to insulation values. Obviously the only steady metabolic states shown in the table are for sleeping and sitting. They're not steady, but they're close enough. The others represent a range of activity that varies from shuffling around camp while chow's being made to scrambling up a steep, short slope with a heavy pack. The insulation suitable for camp is obviously too thick for scrambling. If you tried to scramble in it, you'd be soaking wet in no time and your camp insulation effectively ruined. This means that you have to pack two distince levels of insulation for your waking activities, and one of them must be very flexible and easily modified and adjusted to different heat-producing activities. I've ski-toured on a still, sunny day at 10°F in a fishnet shirt— until a big cloud and a light wind sent me scrambling for a mountain parka damned fast. The same will happen to you many times in winter.

This should give you a clue. If your normal range of activity runs from fairly low level to very high, it's imperative that the layer next to your hide be easily ventilated. Nothing I've used works better than a fishnet shirt. I've worn them of cotton, cotton and polyester, and of wool. While the cotton gets wet faster, it's still a sufficiently open weave (3/8-inch or larger holes; smaller is useless) to be effective. The cotton/polyester blend dries more readily. The wool has smaller openings, and doesn't ventilate quite as well, but on a cold day, it's...well, it feels like wool. It dries with body heat, and doesn't get clammy. Hail to the sheep! I've worn the wool net over a cotton net or a cotton/polyester net at times, and find it an admirable combination under a shell parka or under a wool shirt—or under both if it's really cold.

It's obvious that you can ventilate a bunch of holes tied together with string fairly easily. And you can unbutton your shirt and your cuffs. You can remove your mitten liners and hike in your mitten shells—or barehanded if you choose. You can unzip your fly. All of these work. But the other key to temperature control is your head. Remember that your body's involuntary mechanisms will keep the head and the torso alive at the expense of the extremities. Under normal circumstances, your scalp and nape account for 15 percent of your heat loss if they're unprotected. At extremely low temperatures, an uncovered head can account for 60 percent of your heat loss. The old adage, *"If your feet are cold, put your hat on,"* is true. A hat that offers a variety of con-figurations from full head coverage to "beanie" coverage, combined with a good, deep parka hood, provides all sorts of adjustment and ventilation.

For example, on a cold day I'll begin walking with a zipped-up parka over an opened wool shirt over a fishnet, and a hat and mittens with liners. The parka hood goes first. Next the hat comes up over my ears. Next, the parka gets un-zipped. Next the parka sleeves get un-Velcroed. Next go the mitten liners. Finally, the parka goes. The hat stays—but I may trade the heavy Balaclava for a lightweight Norwegian wool hat with a tassel called a "Troll hat." At a lunch stop, I redress. If it's still cold, I'll pull on a vest under the mountain parka. At camp, I'll shuck my damp fishnet and put on a dry one (if it is damp), change out my socks (which are always damp), pull on windpants, throw a light sweater over the net, then the shirt, and then a big, thick parka with a deep, insulated hood. Hat and mittens? Of course.

This may be overkill to some experienced winter buffs, but I'm skinny and I sweat easily and heavily. Your physiology may not require as many options of clothing. I can't tell you what's best for you. I can only tell you what's best for me, and outline some general principles.

Ventilation is the chief one. That's how you keep your powder dry!

Ventilation's essential. Granted. Now let's take a look at what we're ventilating—that all-important insulation layer.

The tables—both the QMC's and my more conservative adaptation of them—indicate that you don't require a great deal of insulation when you're moving, if you're not exposed to wind and haven't let yourself get soaking wet with sweat. This means that your primary insulation on the trail will be mostly wool—pants, shirt, underwear, hat, mittens and socks—with some shell garments for wind, water and snow protection if necessary. The total value of this insulation probably won't be as great as that of two men's business suits in terms of thickness, but unlike the business suit, which isn't exactly a rationally conceived protective garment, your winter apparel is highly functional, and protects what needs to be protected.

Why wool? Well, the old saying that wool is warm when wet is true. Now don't go out in a freezing rain in nothing but wool. It will lose a lot of air spaces when it's wet—but not all of them. Wool will dry "from the inside out" if you can cut wind losses to the outside and continue to generate normal body heat. If you can't wear wool, wear Orlon, which also retains some air spaces when wet. Avoid all-cotton garments with the exception of string undershirts—and even these come in wool or polyester. On paper, the Duofold underwear—cotton inside, wool outside—should be uncomfortable. In practice, the drawers work nicely. The shirts, if you're active, are typical crew-neck, long-sleeved shirts that aren't readily ventilatable. I should point out, though, that Duofold makes a "river driver's shirt"—for which read GI underwear tops—with two buttons that permit you to ventilate the shirt to about halfway down your breastbone. They come in all wool and the traditional Duofold cotton inner and wool outer, and I think I'll grow fond of them. I'm fonder of the GI stuff, because it's cheaper, but it's getting harder to find in surplus shops. Other than that, there isn't much difference. I don't have a vendor code book handy, but I'd bet that my GI wool and wool and cotton undershirts came from Duofold anyway. Another underwear material just finding its way into American is nylon pile. Made in Norway by Helly-Hanson and the standard garment of the North Sea fisherman, the material doesn't absorb moisture and is thick and cozy. Again, with a thick undershirt, ventilation may pose a problem unless it's buttoned or zipped.

When you're sitting or shuffling around camp or sleeping, your insulation requirements increase dramatically. Wool, however good it may be as an insulator, isn't very efficient in terms of thickness to weight. The winter hiker needs a very comprehensive lightweight insulation layer that can be easily packed. Such an insulation layer will consist more of dead air chopped into pieces of 1/8 inch or less in thickness than of a dense layer of fibers. The insulation layer will be protected against wind penetration losses by a tough, densely-woven shell inside and out.

For years, down has been the darling of the winter hiker for all convective insulation—vests, jackets, parkas, overpants and sleeping bags. But of late, polyester fiberfill in either continuous filament or shopped staple configuration has taken a bite out of the down market.

I'm not going to get involved in any great screaming hassles about down versus synthetics. Neither am I going to examine down plumule by plumule and write a text on the subtle and mostly meaningless distinctions between goose down and duck down. If you're an equipment freak who dotes on distinctions that don't buy you one degree of protection in the field, you won't like what I have to say. If you're interested in finding out how and why things work—y'all come!

DOWN

With the exception of some commercially insignificant amounts of high quality down coming from Canada and the Dakotas, down is an import item. Most of it comes from the Orient, a smaller amount comes from northern Europe. Down is a byproduct of the raising of ducks and geese for slaughter, with one exception, eiderdown, which is hand-gathered from the nests of eider ducks, an Arctic species. Needless to say, eiderdown is harrowingly expensive and excessively rare. If you're lucky enough to have Great Grandma's eiderdown comforter, you have one valuable piece of needlework!

Down comes into the processor's shop in massive bales. It is, at that point, incredibly foul stuff, so it's steam-cleaned in big rotating drums which helps to remove some crud, and then it's sterilized. Next, the dry down is blown into something that works like a fractionating column. The finest plumules are vacuumed off at the top; the coarser ones and small feathers in the middle; the big feathers near the bottom. The residue simply falls with a thud. The down is then blended to conform to several different grades, which are defined by ratio of down to feathers, oil content, resiliency, and, most importantly, filling power. Filling power is simply a measurement of how much volume one ounce of down will occupy.

Way back when, you could find northern European down that came from mature geese raised in a cold climate that would blow up to 700 cubic inches per ounce. No more will you find that kind of down at your friendly local outfitter's. The size of geese grown for market has dropped in recent years, because the folks over there aren't feeding huge families any more—and a 12 pound goose doesn't produce the dense, fluffy down plumules of a big old 25 pound honker. The small amount of prime quality down available on the market is used as blending down now, to raise the loft and resiliency of the run-of-the-mill (run-of-the-bird?) stuff to acceptable (500-525 in. ^{3} filling power per ounce) levels.

As to the duck down versus goose down brouhaha that all outdoor writers are enamoured of explaining, I'll say, without fear of contradiction, that goose down comes from a goose and duck down from a duck—and that your "goose down" bag or jacket may contain goose feathers, duck down, and duck feather in some proportions. There are differences, of course. The best goose down has more filling power than the best duck down, but the best duck down, in turn, has more filling power than average goose down. The distinction is academic in the sense that both will result in a garment that's thick for its weight, compresses readily to a small size, rebounds to maximum expansion time and time again, and lasts almost indefinitely with reasonable care. The main point to remember is that you're buying filling power. Expect to pay more for a 500-525 in^3 per ounce down fill—be it duck or goose or both—than a 400in^3 per ounce down fill.

The alternative to down is polyester fiberfill insulation. In the past, I had a "show me" attitude about the polyesters. All I can say now is that I've been shown. The polyester insulations—the biggies being Du Pont's *Hollofil II* and Celanese's *PolarGuard*—occupy a bit less volume per unit weight than good down, aren't quite as compressible, and *may* not have the lifespan of good down that's been properly cared for. But...they're far, far lower in cost than even mediocre down, they're easier (and therefore less expensive) to fabricate into finished garments, they absorb essentially no moisture, which means that they can be wrung out or shaken "dry" in the field, and they do not lose their thickness even after complete immersion.

From all we've said about insulation in this chapter, it should be evident that the maintenance of a suitable thickness of dry, still air is the key to insulation. The synthetics are dryable in the field should they get wet, because the fibers themselves are essentially impervious to moisture. Furthermore, the fibers will not collapse when they're wet or damp as down will. The result is highly dependable insulation at moderate cost. Unless you're going on long trips where the extra weight and bulk of the synthetic insulation could prove to be a major impediment, they're well worth your consideration.

As long as we're on the topic, the question inevitably arises as to which of the two major synthetic insulations, *Hollofil II* or *PolarGuard,* is "better." I fear my answer must be, "better for what"? A one-inch blanket of *Polarguard* has the same insulation value as a one-inch thickness of *Hollofil II*—or of dried cowpeas or chopped sorghum for that matter. Let's take a look at how these fibers are made (and what they look like) before they're swathed in nylon. This'll give you some insights as to how they differ and what might be the optimum applications of each.

The individual strands of both of these fibers are made by squeezing a viscous material through a small opening, much in the manner that a spider "spins" its web. In fact, the machine that does this is called a spinnaret. Here the similarity ceases. Du Pont's *Hollofil* is chopped up into short lengths, around seven inches or so, and baled up for shipping. *Polarguard* is twisted in a tow (consider it to be a big rope) as it comes from the spinnaret. The tow is then blown open by air jets, and spread across a moving blanket. The speed of the blanket determines the thickness of the insulation, which is "deposited" as an interlocking batt of continuous filaments.

If there are any significant differences between these two fibers in terms of insulation value, I have yet to be made aware of them. The nature of the products—chopped staple versus continuous filament—results in some distinctions when sewn. We'll check into these when we talk about garments. □

FEET

We can discuss hypothermia for pages and pages, but let's chat about what it all means in terms of what you should wear and do—out there in the boonies, whether for an over-night or a two-hour ramble.

In mild weather, anything above 20° and relatively dry, a fast tour through your closet and your good windshell that you use for summer hiking will do the job. Below that, or in wet cold, the problems require some special solutions.

The first problem is your feet. Unless you're a veritable furnace with the cardiovascular system of a marathon runner, hiking boots just won't make it in cold weather. Remember what a hiking boot is, after all. It's a sturdy protective case for your feet, and it conforms to them to the extent that you can fit one heavy and one light sock between it and you without pinching, chafing or tightness. If you think of insulation correctly—as a thickness of dry, still air—you'll realize very quickly that this arrangement yields little insulation. The boot is relatively thin. The wool socks afford some degree of thickness, but when you walk on them, they get damp and matted. The difference in thermal conductivity between damp wool and dry wool is appalling, and wool is a notably **good** performer when it's wet.

Furthermore, that air space formed by the socks isn't dead air. Every step you take compresses the insulation, which rebounds when your foot leaves the ground. This pumping action circulates air around your feet, which is desirable to remove perspiration, but which is most un-desirable in terms of insulation.

Some folks try to overcome this by jamming in extra socks. The result is both predictable and nasty. The extra socks make the boots fit so snugly that circulation is reduced. As we've already seen, one inevitable physiological conse-quence of cold weather is a diminution of blood flow to the extremities, which is why your hands and feet are the first to feel the chill on a brisk day. Tight boots resulting from extra socks further inhibit circulation, and the autonomic processes of the body throttle down the blood supply to the feet even more. The result is still colder feet, which results, again, in a further reduction of blood flow. The end of this process is frostbite.

Clearly, a different boot is required for winter hiking. The parameters are easy to define. It should be large enough to accommodate two pairs of heavy socks (with one exception which we'll note later); it should provide a waterproof protective barrier for your insulation layer or provide for a readily renewable insulation layer; it should be high enough to keep snow out of the inside without gaiters if the snow depth isn't enough to make gaiters mandatory, and it should be comfortable.

For some unaccountable reason, the hiker has seen fit to learn from the mountaineer alone, and sedulously avoid, if not despise, the wisdom of the hunter and the trapper, both of whom operate in conditions more related to hiking than does the big mountain climber. I'm as anomaly, perhaps. I came to hiking and backpacking and paddling from fishing and hunting and trapping as a kid—which is a roundabout way of saying that I grew up in shoepacs. You know the kind. Relatively high leather uppers, rubber "feet", heavy crepe soles, and thick felt innersoles. (Yes, you carried a spare pair of innersoles and socks, particularly if you were running a trapline. To do otherwise was to risk almost instant frostbite from a misstep on thin ice.) There are lots of these boots on the market today, but when I was a kid, the best—the most durable, the most well made, the most comfortable, and the only rebuildable—shoepac was the venerable L. L. Bean Maine Hunting Shoe. As the fella says, "Ain't nothin' much has changed". The Bean Boot still works, and you can order it out in an appropriate size to fit over your socks with absolute assurance that the folks in Freeport will come up with an appropriate fit, most always on the first shot.

Of course, the Bean Boot and its imitators depend on a renewable insulation layer for maintaining warmth. Extra socks are a necessity, as is an extra set of innersoles. I had three sets of both as a kid. One I wore, one I carried as an emergency pair, and one was drying on the rack behind the stove in my uncle's kitchen. I remember that stove with fondness. Like most farms of the time, most of the cooking was done on a modern stove—in this case electric—in a sub-kitchen/pantry room. The old wood stove was a constant source of heat for the big kitchen and the rooms overhead, a supplier of baked goods, coffee and stew, and home for an

Irish setter and three overfed cats—and I'd like to find one like it today for my farmhouse kitchen!

But that's beside the point. Three sets of renewable insulation isn't, though. It's a useful system because it guarantees one spare set that's always there and always dry.

The shoepac has changed through the years. Not all of them resemble the venerable Bean Boot. In fact, the Bean Boot has changed—at least one model of it. Let's look at some of the other possibilities.

First, of course, is the ubiquitous shoepac with a felt liner, the commonest of which is the Canadian-made Sorel boot. The leather-uppered, rubber-footed Sorel with a full-length inner boot of felt is warm. It isn't as neatly conforming around the ankles and shins as the Bean boot, which means that you'll get snow inside if you don't take proper measures. It isn't as comfortable for long treks, but it is warm, relatively inexpensive, and the insulation layer—the felt inner boot—is quickly exchanged in the field if it gets wet. A further advantage of this system is that the felt liners can be worn by themselves as tent booties, or, when protected by a coated nylon overboot, as camp booties. I've beefed up a pair of the cheapest Sorel boots with an innersole of 3/8-inch Ensolite, and after I slip the felt inner boot in place and wriggle my dogs into it, with a couple of pairs of socks, I'm set for just about anything up to and including a day of ice fishing, which can make a hard trek in the high country seem like a Victorian garden party. You don't believe me? Try it sometime!

Most books you'll find on winter hiking—for which read "mountaineering"—sing the praises of the GI surplus winter boots, the white "Mickey Mouse" boot or the black Korean boot often called the "black mouse" or the "K-boot". I'm not about to demean the mouse boot. It's just that the genuine article is virtually impossible to find, and of such an age that the rubber may be suspect. The black boot was designed for wet cold use, and the Army Quartermaster Corps defined it as a -20°F boot with the recommended one pair of cushion-soled 50% wool 50% cotton socks. The white boot was defined as warm to -65° F (inactive) and -85° F active, again with one pair of cushion-soled socks. Yep, you read that last set of figures right. Minus 65 and minus 85. The secret, as it were, is that the insulation layer around the foot and ankle is both thick and completely sealed, like a vacuum bottle. It can't get wet unless the boot is punctured, and air can't circulate around inside it. The socks are there for comfort and perspiration absorption; you'd be just as warm without them.

There's that lesson again. You can be wet if your *insulation* is dry. Your feet will get soaked in mouse boots. You'll wring out your socks and pour sweat out of your boots after a long trek, but that thick, still blanket of dry air will keep you warm.

The mouse boot has created a host of imitations, some excellent and some downright shabby. Bean (again!) does an insulated version of the venerable Maine Hunting Shoe that's what you'd expect from Bean, and some of the big outdoor footgear outfits like Converse and Red Ball produce all-rubber "vacuum-bottle" boots that are very good. Some cheap boots are around that look as good, but have a disarming tendency to fail in service. Remember, a crack or a split in the outer or inner of a sealed-insulation boot will admit moisture to the insulation, and the boot is dead as far as warmth goes. The cheap boots tend to crack at low temperatures, which isn't very nice of them at all!

A recent development of the QMC, now in limited commercial availability, is a vacuum-bottle boot with an insulation layer of flexible closed-cell foam. Light, sturdy, and not subject to significant moisture absorption or significant air circulation if the inner or outer "skins" are ruptured, this boot looks like the answer to the cold weather lover's prayers. I haven't tried a pair as yet, but I'm inclined to listen when the QMC talks, because they don't talk notions or opinions. They talk numbers and test data and field data based on huge samples. If they say that such and such a configuration will keep 95 percent of the troops warm in the following combinations of temperature and humidity (assuming adequate rations), you can believe it.

There are other factors that come into play with winter boot selection. An insulation system that works in one mode may be a dismal flop in another. For example, on a cold, dry, day, I'll snowshoe in mukluks, the old white canvas GI jobs with leather soles. I'll slip in a felt inner sole and pull on two pairs of heavy socks and tromp around. But not in steep terrain. If I'm webbing in steep terrain, I'll be wearing my little aluminum snowshoes (Sherpas, in case you're curious) with a heavy binding on them that was designed for wear with climbing boots. The mukluks are warm enough, but the binding compresses the very soft insulation system enough to be uncomfortable. I'll wear different boots with them. But for low-country rambling for a few hours with a long, skinny pair of webs, the mukluks are fine. They're light, flexible and easy to lope in.

If, on the other hand, I was climbing an Adirondack peak where I might be walking on a packed-out trail for a while, snowshoeing for a while, and scrambling up steep, .icy windslab for a while, I'd need a boot that was sufficiently supportive for walking and that could be fitted with crampons for safety on the icy, packed junk on the summit ridge. Mukluks wouldn't make it. Neither would a lot of otherwise useful winter boots. At that point, I'd opt for the mouse boot, which will accept a crampon, or an insulated shoepac with a lug sole—both of which are less than optimum for snowshoeing.

What I'm really getting around to mentioning is that there are precious few absolutes in equipment selection on a broad scale. **You** ultimately have to decide on what you'll be doing the most of. If lowland cruising is your delight, your boots should reflect this. If you're a high-country denizen, and snowshoeing steep terrain—or an Easterner who's enamored of peakbagging—you'll need something more specialized that isn't as much fun to romp in on a casual cruise in the back woodlot. But only you know what you want to do.

By the way, if this sounds expensive, or if you only want to go out a few times for jaunts in the winter on snowshoes, there is an alternative approach that works for easy going. Overshoes! Old five-buckle Arctics'! You may have a pair around the house; you may find a pair at the Salvation Army or Goodwill Industries store; you may have to resort to buying them, perish the thought. But—a felt inner boot liner (called a "snowmobile boot liner" by a lot of shops), a felt innersole and the old overshoes will make a light, dry, warm combination for low-country slogging. A hint here—overshoes are meant (obviously) to be worn over street shoes, which means that the heel is distinctly lower than you'll probably like. Fill the heel cavity with felt or foam, and you'll be ready to roam. And for the record, the overshoe game is great for kids. It results in a much warmer boot for the money than the Korean or Taiwanese-made "insulated" boots that most kids freeze in every winter.

Now that you've gotten your boot requirements squared away, let's look at some ways to keep deep snow out of those boots when you're on the trail. I should point out that snow obeys the First Law of the Perverse. If it's two inches deep, it will contrive a way to be two feet deep at a spot you choose to stand in after removing your gaiters. Or, you'll contrive to nudge a snow-laden branch in such a fashion as to get a neckful and a bootful of the freaky, cold stuff at the same time. Or you'll fall. Or something. I have. Almost every time out, in fact, and while I'm no gazelle, I'm no more than average clumsy. If you, like me, put your pants on one leg at a time, be assured that you'll get a bootful of snow if you don't take precautions.

The precautions come in several forms: gaiters, over-pants, and overboots. The commonest—and least expensive—is gaiters, which are nothing more than pantslegs of nylon or 60/40 cloth ranging from 6 to 18 inches long, generally closed by a zipper or zipper and snaps, and grommeted so that they can be fastened snugly under the in-step with a cord or strap. In some circles, discussion about gaiters can be hot and heavy, chiefly over whether or not the gaiters should be of a "breathable" material—that is, whether they should transmit perspiration away from your shanks, and, at the same time, transmit snowmelt in the other direc-tion. I'll concede that the breathable gaiter is more comfor-table, but only when the weather is reasonably warm and the snow is wet—precisely when I need protection against melting snow. I like waterproof gaiters, preferably knee-high, but then I don't run on a day trip, and I don't overdress in general—which means that I don't sweat a lot. Experiment on your own. Most winter buffs have several pairs of gaiters, and if you go on your first full-day outing with one of them (and I recommend this highly), maybe you can borrow a pair and try one variety for yourself. If it works—and chances are that it will, coated or uncoated—go get something like it. The key, of course, is to **do it.** If you spend your winter in endless debate about optimum equipment, your outfitter will get rich at your expense. You won't ever get out and see first hand what's there. Remember, some incredible winter trips have been recorded in North America by folks who were remarkably ill-equipped by contemporary standards. Granted, it's debatable whether those people enjoyed themselves, and you're going out there for pleasure rather than the necessity of making a living, but to fret about op-timization is to spend all your time reading catalogs and books in front of the fire. This is fine, but don't confuse it with winter hiking.

Overboots are gaiters with feet, and they're absolute essentials if you're doing serious climbing where crampons are a necessity. They're intended to be worn over mountaineering boots, and they do the job if the weather isn't extreme. Of course the serious mountaineer probably has a pair of double boots, which are mountain boots with an inner lace-up boot of felt or of glove leather with insulation. The few times I've used overboots have been with regular mountain boots on some of the pacific Northwest firepeaks, and they kept me dry and added just enough warmth—probably by keeping me dry—that my feet were cozy when most of the party was complaining about cold feet.

Overpants are a wholly different consideration. These are worn primarily for wind protection—or for wind and wet snow protection—in rather more rugged conditions than the average winter hiker will choose to encounter. I wouldn't dream of going above timberline without overpants in my pack, and I'll often carry them in the lowlands to slip on while I'm eating lunch to cut down wind losses and to reduce the hassle of wet knees or a wet butt from crouching in the snow or sitting on a log. They're usually long enough to keep snow out of your boots—but I still wear gaiters with mine! I suspect that overpants are superfluous for the low-country tripper—but I like 'em. They weigh next to nothing, and provide an amazing amount of protection. □

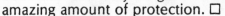

HANDS

I've always deplored the type of winter hiking book that spends so much time talking about the horrible things that can happen in the cold that you wonder if it was written more to convince the reader that the writer is a real macho dude than it was to inform him. However, there are hazards involved in winter hiking that have to be considered, and there have been times when some grisly tradeoffs have been made in the name of survival. Proper preparation and a modicum of good sense will make these tradeoffs mere objects of speculation—but consider this for a second: If you had to walk out of a winter incident, and you could protect either your hands or your feet from severe frostbite that might well result in the loss of toes or fingers, what would you choose to protect? The obvious—and wrong—answer is your feet. You **can** walk on badly frostbitten feet; there is nothing you can do to provide food for yourself, or even light a match, with frostbitten hands. Hand protection is important. If you're not in a survival situation—and chances are that you never will be unless you choose to be—warm, cozy hands are simply more pleasant and far more useful than cold ones. Ever try to do any fussy little task with really cold hands? Like light a stove, or prepare a meal, or even adjust snowshoe bindings? Or, on simple terms, even unlock the car door on a day when you forgot your gloves? The most elementary task becomes hideously complex with cold hands.

The backcountry is no place to be with wet mittens or skimpy dress gloves, my friend. Let's look at the whole problem of hand protection, beginning with the statement that gloves are useless except for short-term protection while performing fussy chores.

Hands are difficult to insulate, and fingers even more so. The extremities are subject to reduced blood flow in general, and that flow will be throttled by the body in cold weather to preserve heat in the torso. Further, the hands, like the feet, are righly endowed with sweatglands, which means that insulation will get damp easily. As a final indignity, the weight of a pack tends to constrict blood flow to the arms and hands, too—and the winter hiker is probably carrying more than he

33

would for the same trip in summer. All in all, it's obvious that your hands need help.

I have a few prejudices in hand protection. One is that I like wool mittens; another is that I always carry at least one extra pair in my pack; finally, I prefer an overmitt with a long gauntlet-like cuff to protect against snow and wind. In warmer weather, or when I'm skiing, I like those heavy leather shell mitts called "chopper" mitts, but for heavy going, I like the heavy nylon overmitts with gauntlet cuffs. I've used down mittens, the fancy jobs with nosewipers on the back, and for bitter cold, particularly around camp or in static situations, they surely do the job, but they're too warm for most lowcountry situations. They're useless when wet, and provide no degree of flexibility. The woolen mitten and overshell combination is particularly useful in those situations where the temperature is chilly enough to warrant the protection afforded by insulation until your body is on the line enough to generate some warmth, at which time you can peel off the combination, stuff the not-yet-damp woolen mitts in your pocket, and wear the shells along for wind protection and protection against snow. The key to this—indeed the key to keeping warm and dry—is to remove clothing before you start to sweat and replace it before you get cold.

If you'll forgive a minor digression, the first bicycle "boom" in Europe, at around the turn of the century, had as its principal spokesman a French workman named Paul de Vivie, who wrote much and well under the pen name of Velocio. He formulated seven rules for the bicycle tourist that are applicable to all self-propelled pursuits from kayaking to snowshoeing.

1. Eat **before** you're hungry.
2. Drink **before** you're thirsty.
3. Peel off **before** you're sweaty.
4. Put back on **before** you're chilly.
5. Rest **before** you're tired.
6. Don't use tobacco or alcohol on a tour.
7. Don't tour just to prove that you can do it.

Right there, in a nutshell, is a textbook on winter hiking—and we'll be talking about all of those things in many different contexts. At this point, remember that you can't keep your mittens dry if you wear them when you're sweating. Take 'em off and put them where they'll **stay** dry and wear the shells alone—or go barehanded if it's comfortable. Replace your hand protection at the first inkling of discomfort or chill.

I'm somewhat of an old woodchuck. When I was a kid, I rubbed my hands with a tallow and balsam mixture to kill my scent on a trap and to afford a degree of protection againt wet snow and wind. I still do, only now I use Vaseline or a balsam and beeswax compound made up for bowhunters, who face the problem of sitting still for hours in chilly weather with a hunting weapon that must be used barehanded. Does it work? I can't say for sure—but I'll use it on my hands and on my nose and cheeks until I'm too feeble to go into the winter woods. It feels like it works, at any rate—and it definitely cuts down on windburn. Try it yourself. You may like it.

Lightweight gloves are useless for warmth, as I've indicated. In fact, heavyweight gloves are useless, too. You simply can't pack enough insulation around your fingers in that configuration to be of much value. However, light gloves can be most useful for lighting a stove, handling a camera, adjusting a snowshoe binding, burrowing into your pack or pitching a tent—in short, for any **short-term** use that requires a measure of finger dexterity. Some people swear by ultrathin silk, nylon or rayon gloves, which they wear as inner liners under their mittens or shells for just such purposes. They do work, but I'd rather dig mine out of my parka pocket. And I use cheap cotton work-gloves that I've sprayed the dickens out of with a water-repellent for most of these tasks. I prefer mittens for tentpitching and stove filling (if not stove lighting).

Stoves require a note here as well as in the "right" place. A winter stove is a gasoline stove. Accept that for now as gospel. Gasoline is a fluid that can be supercooled. Its freezing point is savagely low. If you're filling a stove on a -20°F day, that fuel is at -20°F. To spill it on your hands is to invite instant frostbite. **Don't handle gasoline on a cold day without hand protection.** Period. Don't even grab the container without hand protection.

Earlier I knocked the big fat down expedition mittens, and I should clarify this a bit. There are times when situations are so extreme that down (or synthetic) expedition mitts are absolutely essential, and I'll find room for a pair of them on a trip that might promise some bitter weather or long, exposed treks above timberline. For the casual valley rambler, they're superfluous. If you really suffer from chilly extremities—and some folks do—that's another matter. Then I'd consider the big mitts—but I'd be more inclined to choose a synthetic mitt (*Polarguard* or *Fiberfill II*) that will hold up to moisture better than down.

A few more hints on warm hands before we move on. No mitten is worth a damn if you lost it two miles back on the trail. I carry extra mittens, and they're snug and secure in my pack. If I peel off the shells, they go in the pack too, or in a secure pocket in my parka along with the mittens I've been wearing. Under no circumstances should you casually lash your shells to the pack because they're damp. Losing them could be a real bummer. In really cold weather, where you're wearing either down or synthetic Mighty Mitts or the big Army surplus Korea mitts or a shell with *two* pairs of mittens under it, you should either secure each mitt to a parka sleeve with nylon tape and a safety pin, or play the game that Mommy did when you were a kid, which is to run a long piece of nylon tape from one mitt up your sleeve, across your back and down the other sleeve to the other mitt. Loss of hand protection in a situation where you require an expedition mitt could leave you nicknamed "Stumpy". Needless to say, you still carry the basic shell and woolen mitt combination even if you plan on using Mighty Mitts most of the time. □

FOOD

In *Movin' Out,* I spent one page on food for the three-season backpacker and nine pages on cooking gear and the care and feeding of small stoves. My premise was that the temperate-weather hiker needs to consider food as a frill, if you will. We are, generally, overfed, over-vitamined and overweight, and none of us will starve on a two day trip. The intimation, simply stated, was "eat what you like." In the course of the book, I probably spent more time discussing water than food.

Winter is a whole 'nother smoke, friends. You're a heat engine. A lot of other things, too, but those things don't matter for now. Many of you are brave, many of you are fair of countenance, many of you are wise—and all of you are ambulatory engines: all of you need fuel. And you need more of it in winter than in summer.

Why? Your body is happiest at 98.6°F give or take a few tenths. It maintains optimum temperature, in part, by "burning" food. When the body runs out of fuel "in the tank," as it were, it taps stored food; first the liver, then the fatty tissues. In extremities, it cheerfully consumes muscle tissue.

However, this isn't a primer on physiology. It's a book about how to be comfortable, even ecstatic, in winter. And part of winter ecstasy depends on food.

Food for the winter traveler is rather a more complex subject than it is for the summer timber trotter. Water has to be melted, generally, and the expenditure of fuel and time is considerable. Yet it's dangerous to neglect this task and subsist on munchies that require no water in their preparation, because dehydration dramatically reduces your resistance to cold, increases your chances of frostbite, and at high elevations, contributes markedly toward acute mountain sickness. I'm a lowlander, but I've been in high country in cold weather enough to notice several phenomena. First is that thirst is less apparent in winter generally, and even less apparent at 10,000 feet and above. Second is that I'm a compulsive guzzler of water in winter, and I'm generally far warmer than my non-guzzling brethren who view my fluid intake as pure self-indulgence. Granted, these observations aren't very scientific, but they seem to be supported in the literature of high-altitude medicine. Eat your no-cooking munchies if you will—but wash them down with a lot of water, cocoa, coffee, tea, lemonade or whatever strikes your fancy. My own preference is Wyler's lemonade and tea mixed half and half with a big gob of margarine thrown in for the sheer old fat joy of it.

In simplest terms, the winter hiker lives on a diet of leaf lard and sugar. Fats and carbohydrates are the fuels you most crave, although a lot of people misinterpreted an Army QMC document of a few years ago and assumed it said that humans don't **require** fat in a cold environment. In fact it said that most of the test subjects (soldiers, a random selection thereof) didn't display the "fat hunger" spoken of in the past by hard-core Arctic and boreal forest wanderers. This doesn't imply that they didn't require fats in their diet; one could almost be a wiseacre and say that if they were typical young American males, they had stored enough fat to not feel a fat hunger for some months.

Howbeit, one of my favorite winter trail snacks, the ingredients of which will turn the stomach of a healthy stercoricolous microorganism, is a mixture of butter, powdered eggs, powdered milk, sugar and vanilla, with a little peanut butter thrown in if I'm in the mood. It keeps indefinitely in the cold, provides an awesome 2600 or so calories per pound and tastes just great on a cold day. Just like cookie dough—which, as you may have noticed, it really is. The exact recipe is 3 ounces of powdered whole egg, 3 ounces of non-fat dried milk, 8 ounces of butter, 5 ounces of confectioner's sugar, and vanilla to taste. Add peanut butter if you wish, but try it with a small chunk of the original. The basic mix isn't mine. It's a concoction of Gerry Cunningham's, and I've always considered it to be one more of a long list of things that all backpackers are indebted to Gerry for. So much for "fat hunger." I believe in it—and nibble accordingly.

If winter cookery can be a hassle due to short daylight hours, heavy fuel requirements, numb fingers, numb feet and the fact that most foods congeal to an ugly, tepid mass before they can be eaten, it also has some distinct advantages. Refrigeration is no problem. Goodies can be carried in winter that couldn't be toted in summer. The stew you spill in winter can be scooped from the clean bed of snow on which it fell and shoveled back into the pot with impunity. And there's an urgency to your appetite that fairly makes you drool. After all, you need about 1000 more calories a day in winter than in summer to break even on the heat balance equation, and that's only a part of it. You're carrying more, and working harder.

Planning a menu for a group is never easy, but winter imposes limitations that may make the task more complex if you have a lot of fussbudgets in your party. Assume the following:

- You need lots cf food to cope with a high level of activity.
- You may be faced with severe weather conditions that make meal preparation very difficult.
- You will, in all probability, have to cook and eat in a hurry, due to a combination of poor light, cold hands, cold feet and food that cools quickly.
- You will generally have to melt snow for water—and a safe intake per person is between a quart and a quart and a half per fifty pounds of body weight. That's safe. Comfortable is rather more.
- Firebuilding, if not forbidden by law or by ethical considerations, is not easy in winter. You can't depend on fire for melting snow or for warmth.

Those are the givens. They mandate certain approaches and solutions.

- If the meal can't be cooked in one pot and kept hot while everybody dips up many small portions that will stay palatably warm, chances are it isn't worth preparing.
- Use of convenience foods that will cut down preparation time in bad weather is advisable. You don't need to build a trip menu around them, but one serving per person of something like a Mountain House "just add boiling snowmelt and eat" dish kept in reserve for that particularly lousy night is a fine idea that won't gain you a *cordon bleau* but will earn you the applause of your intrepid snow sluggers. (Actually, I dote on Mountain House franks and beans, and have used it as a staple for either breakfast or dinner on several long solo trips, alternating it with their chile con carne. I know, smart guy! With that sort of diet, it was inevitable that I'd be hiking alone. No, not really. I like beenieweenie; that's all.)
- Anything you can premix in a plastic bag, or mix in a plastic bag at the campsite, is preferable to anything that requires being stirred in a dish or a pot, or mixed up from scratch. For example, if you're a hot cereal chomper in the morning, dump the cereal, sugar, powdered milk and fruit

39

together **at home** so you don't have to fuss with it in the morning.

- Enrich everything that's remotely enrichable. Toss some crunchy-munchies like sesame seeds or peanuts into the cereal mix. Double the sugar in everything with sugar in it. Double the powdered milk (but not the water) in the cereal. Be lavish with margarine, and be particularly lavish with it in cereal, stews and tea.
- Use the quickest-cooking form of whatever it is you're eating. Quick-cooking rice may be an abomination compared to brown rice, but your karma will survive the shock, and you won't have a vitamin crisis from two days of less than organic food. If you're unsure of this, pop a vitamin pill. Just so long as you don't waste the precious (and heavy!) fuel to feed your whims.
- All meals should be labeled with indelible ink or laundry marker or tape, with instructions clear enough that any member of the party can prepare them.
- All members of the party must be able to erect any tent or shelter being used, and be able to make the party's stove stand up and whistle "Hail to the Chief" in a high wind at -10°F.
- You have to either pack fuel to create water for rehydration of freeze-dried food or carry the food with water or oil in it—and it's just about a tradeoff in weight. Certain meals should be carried that require no cooking at all for truly nasty weather. Canned tuna fish (in oil), sardines, Triscuit or Ry-Krisp or pilot biscuit, dried fruit, Gerry's Superdough— things you can chomp down while on the march or eat in your sleeping bag while the snow melts grudgingly in the vestibule.
- Your stove is your mainstay and your ever-present buddy in time of danger. Make sure that yours is in tip-top shape before you leave, and carry a back-up stove, which can be a little dude, preferable an Optimus 8R with a mini-pump. I'll tell you why later.

Start the kitchen equipment considerations with the stove, or for a longer trip, the stoves. The backup stove is handy to keep a supply of water melting (or to cool over while the big stove is roaring away at the snow), and it can serve as a backup if the big stove fails or the party has to split up to seek emergency evacuation for an injured member. There are several stoves that could be useful as the main stove for a party: the Optimus 111B, the big Phoebus 625 and the MSR. I've heard good things about the new Coleman, and Tom Decker, an experienced mountaineer and an accurate reporter, gave it an excellent bill of health in *Wilderness Camping*, but I haven't used it yet in winter. I have used the other three. I'll concede that the MSR is probably the most efficient of the lot, but I prefer the 111B and the Phoebus, becuase I'm simply more familiar with them, and I still don't like having to chase parts for the MSR by mail. Pressed for a choice, I'd probably have to go with the 111B because I like its stability in snow— but mostly because I've used mine so long that I can field-strip the thing in a dark tent and reassemble it. This isn't intended to be a put-down of the Phoebus 625, which is a screaming blowtorch of a stove, but after ten years of association with my 111B, and a lot of meals whipped together in trying conditions, I can only say that it's achieved the status of trail mate.

My choice for backup stove would come from a group of three: The Optimus 8R with mini-pump, the Phoebus 725 and the Enders Benzin Baby. The mini-pump makes a winter stove out of the little self-generating 8R. It's not a high-output stove—not nearly as hot as the 725 or the Enders—but it's all of a piece with nothing to assemble or lose, and it's very, very stable, which I like. Stability, or lack of it, is why I wouldn't consider the Svea 123 for serious winter use, and I think that the 8R is enough more stable than the 725 to offset the 725's higher output. Both of these stoves, by the way, are quite efficient in wind. The little Enders, a unique small pressurized stove, is a joy and a delight and very efficient—and all its parts have to be assembled to use it. Someday I'll figure out how to wire them together and snap them into place, but a lost throttle key puts you out of business. And in case you didn't know it, it's easy to lose things in snow.

I realize that choosing stoves is rather like choosing classical recordings—there's much to be said for almost any version in the rack. And I further realize that my objection to the MSR—that I can't find parts for it at most outfitters—is unreasonable in light of the fact that MSR responds very quickly to mail orders, makes a massive effort to retrofit stoves if it looks like a part is failing more often than they'd like, and makes improvements available to owners of old stoves at a reasonable price. It's just that I'm the sort of dude who decides he needs a new pump leather in Big Blue Box at 8:30

on Friday night, so I can leave early Saturday, and it's 25 minutes by car to my favorite backpacking shop, which closes at 9:00. I can't do that with an MSR. Of course, I could order out a few bucks worth of spare parts and keep them around the house, which is what a sensible person would do, but...

For cooking gear, I'd take one pot with a lid and a generously-sized teapot like the Trangia or Hope, or two nesting pots with lids. One of them must have a bail (or be a teapot). Why? Often you'll find a stream running a tiny trickle, but it's fifteen feet down a steep, unstable wall of snow. So you go water fishing. For that, you need parachute cord, a pot with a bail (or a teapot), and a ski pole or an ice axe. It's a hassle—but less of a hassle than melting snow, and it tastes better. Sure, I know that that water is nothing more than melted snow, but somehow melted snow always tastes like... well, melted snow. You can actually **scorch** the damn stuff. Scorched snowmelt tastes sort of like a scorched pillowcase smells. And that does nothing to enhance the vanilla pudding, believe me.

I eat out of a Sierra cup with a tablespoon. An insulated plastic mug might be better—but I can put the Sierra cup (mine says SMC on it, not Sierra Club) back on the stove and warm some life back into the coffee. Try that with polystyrene!

I tote a pot hook (or two, if I have two pots), a small bottle of biodegradable soap (which I rarely use), a scrubby pad (mine's called a Dobie, I think), and a couple of plastic bags for trash and one (the dark variety) to collect water with on a sunny day if I'm in a base camp. How? Find an open spot sheltered from the wind, spread out your bag so it's in the form of an inverted shallow cone (punch it down in the middle), spread snow over it and go off exploring. You'll find water when you return, if you don't wait till sundown.

I also carry some scraps of Ensolite. Actually, they weren't scraps. I cut down a long pad once and kept the piece, which I cut up 1) to fit under the stoves, 2) to fit under my behind or under my feet or under my knees, and 3) to wrap around a packet of Mountain House beenieweenie to keep the little mother warm while it's reconstituting.

Another item you might consider is a firesheet. I don't usually bother with a fire because it's simply too much of a hassle, but if you're in an area where there's an amount of dead wood available, a firesheet is useful. Make it out of a few pieces of aluminum of about 1' x 2', hung together in folding-screen fashion, long edge to long edge, with twisted wire. Hang this just above the snow with wires leading to four ski poles or ice axes or saplings, and you have a firesheet that won't sink out of sight.

All of which brings up another consideration. You know enough (I hope!) not to camp at the base of an avalanche track or under a dead tree or out where the wind can tear at you. Now—don't build your kitchen under a big old honker of a pine tree with snow-laden branches either, because as sure as God made iceworms, a stray breeze will rustle that tree, and if only one slug of snow falls, you can be certain that it'll fall in the stew or on your uncovered head or both. I have. And it has. And it's enough to make a middle-aged reprobate cry!

Some further arrangement of the cooking area is useful. Tromp it (and the tent area) down with your skis or snowshoes, and really stomp down an area around the cook stoves. Pack a little raised shelf for the stoves and other stuff if you can, and take pains to position the stoves securely on their Ensolite footwarmers. The next operation is simple. One cooks; one tends the snowmelt; everybody else puts up the tents. When the tents are up, the tent erectors can scrounge wood or water in its liquid state or sit and shiver—but keep them the hell away from the stoves! Any well-brought-up stove will unhorse its cookpot if given half an excuse, and well-intentioned, cold-handed assistance is rather more than half. Spilling the stew isn't half the tragedy that spilling the water is. The stew can be scooped up and reheated. The water (and the fuel that melted it) is gone, gone, gone.

The other arrangement of the cooking area is that, in my less-than-humble opinion, the cooking area is **outside.** It would require absolute survival conditions to prompt me to cook inside a tent. I have been known to lie in my sleeping bag and reach a mittened hand out of the tunnel opening and cook by remote control as it were in foul weather or when I was particularly chilly from too much trucking and too little eating. Now, I know that a lot of folks cook inside a tent, and I know that a lot of tents come with cookholes. To those facts I can only say 1) cook inside **your** tent, not mine, and 2) cookholes are great places for tossing the dottle from the evening pipeful of Brindley's into, and some less than fastidious souls have been known to urinate in them in the middle of a cold night, but they're not for cooking. Not in my tent.

We've talked a lot about snowmelt, but not about the process of melting snow. To begin with, you're best advised to start with a little bit of water in the pan to avoid scorching the snow. Aha! But how do we get that water? Well, if we've just come from home, it's easy. In really cold weather, you may have to bury your waterbottle inside your pack and wrap it in an Ensolite scrap to insure that it stays unfrozen during the day. At night, the game is played this way. Melt up lots of water, and fill all waterbottles with warm water. Wrap them in Ensolite scraps or a synthetic-insulated vest, and plop them in the bottom of your sleeping bag. If it's not too cold out, wrap them and put them in one pack, all together, and keep that pack in the tent, where it will be about 10°-15° warmer. If you're really cramped for space, maintain at least one small waterbottle per person in sleeping bags. This insures several things: water to start breakfast with, or at least to melt more snow with; water for washing down midnight munchies that keep the metabolic fires roaring; water for washing down an aspirin in case of headache, muscle pains from overexertion or the general blahs that you get at higher elevations if you're less well acclimated, and water to keep your fluid balance at an optimum level. Many times I've woken up chilly at three in the morning and guzzled a pint of water instead of a candy bar. It works, and I'll repeat it again and again. Dehydration in winter is insidious, because you don't feel thirsty. And dehydration increases your chances of falling prey to hypothermia, acute mountain sickness and frostbite.

I haven't said much about trail meals thus far for a couple of reasons. The first is that I choose to assume that you're competent to determine what you prefer to eat without my help. The second is that an Oregon backpacker, June Fleming, has already done much of the work in a little volume called *The Well-Fed Backpacker,* published by Victoria House in Portland. The heart of June's book is a small section called "One-Liners," and the theory of the one-liner meal is simple. Imagine six columns, headed Meat or Meat Substitutes—Pasta, Grains and Other Bases; Vegetables; Sauces; Seasonings, and Toppings, and Extra Additions. Pick one food from each column (Be sure to include one from each of the first three; the other three are optional.) in whatever quantity turns you on, put 'em all together, and stew 'em up. It's not quite that simple, but almost—and the variety is endless, the preparation straightforward, the palatibility excellent, and the nutritional base solid. Furthermore, the bulk of the foods listed are readily available at your friendly local supermarket or natural food store, or you can home-dry a lot of them yourself with a low-cost dryer that she tells you how to make.

Let's take a look at a few specimen one-liners out of the over 700,000 combinations you can create from June's lists.

Rice - baconbar - dried tomato - pepper and onion flakes - cheese sauce

Potato - meat bar - vegetable soup mix - gravy mix

Potato au gratin - green beans - tuna - cheese sauce

Spinach noodles - sliced sausage - sour cream mix - parmesan cheese

See how it goes? You could even create your lists to suit your own tastes. Just remember that the demands of the winter environment require that you select the quickest-cooking items. Quick-cooking brown rice is available; regular brown rice would require too much fuel and time. Quick-cooking spaghetti is available. If you can't find it, buy the thinnest spaghetti you can find and break it up for cooking. You have to do a little thinking to prepare these meals beforehand, however, in terms of organizing things in order of cooking time. For example, one of my old-time staples is a conglomeration of vegetable beef soup mix with half of the water the packet calls for, some freeze-dried green beans, a whiff of gravy mix, and meat bar. I may flesh it out by sauteeing some small chunks of turnip (which travel well in winter) in the pan before I dump in the soup and the water, and I'll probably throw in some onion and pepper flakes and maybe even some more dried potato with the soup. If I do, I'll add a little more water to the soup mix. The beans go in with the soup, and the meat bar and gravy mix can be dumped in later, along with a lump of margarine. The whole thing takes 15 minutes, is made in one pot, can be kept hot while everybody dips up a small ration and wolfs it down, and it fills in around the edges, particularly if you eat some pilot biscuit with it.

Cleanup is simple. To begin with, there usually isn't anything left. I wipe the pan with snow (a marvelous scrubbing pad, by the way, and always available), pour in more water, and brew up tea. Sometimes I'll brew up the tea without cleaning up the pot. If you add enough sugar, powdered milk and margarine to the tea, you hardly notice the onion flakes!

So much for supper. Breakfast is probably the most troublesome meal in that it's always cold out, and it takes an act of will to get out of the sack and start melting snow. Of course, you have some water already available hiding in the bottom of your sleeping bag, and you have a good chunk of packed, dense snow from the night before to melt. Melting nice fluffy powder is like pouring sand in a rat-hole. Pack down a neat little heap of snow the night before, and make sure you pack enough for breakfast. Get the water warmed up, and scoop a cupful of snow into it. When that melts down, add another cupful, and so on. If you start with very little water, add snow in small amounts, otherwise the snow will absorb it all and you'll wind up scorching the snow. I know. You don't believe me? Try it sometime. It's repulsive!

I'm a believer in a basic breakfast—hot cereal with fruit, powdered milk, powdered egg, peanut butter and margarine stirred into it, and eaten sort of "wet," followed by all the hot drinks I can absorb, up to and including hot Jell-O, which beats hell out of fruit juice. Take the time to melt enough snow to top up all water bottles, and keep topping them up as you drink whenever "free" water is available along the route. If I sound like a fanatic about water, it's because I am. And I got that way by experience.

Lunch begins after breakfast is finished. Big fat trail cookies, Gorp, dried fruits, Gerry's Superdough, nuts, seeds—you name it. The key to maintaining your energy level is to eat **before** you're hungry, remember? And to drink **before** you're thirsty. Keep those goodies in a parka pocket or in a belt pouch that you can get at easily, and keep on chewin' while you keep on truckin'. A formal lunch break is useful. You might even break out the big stove and brew up some tea if there's water nearby, in the honored tradition of the cruisers of the boreal forests. They called it a "mug-up," and they tried to have one every couple of hours. Trappers, prospectors, hunters they were—hard-nosed, seasoned outdoors people. They knew what they were doing!

As an aside, I submit a book by Calvin Rustrum to your attention—*Paradise Below Zero*. A lot of modern backpackers scorn it because of its intransigently "old-timey" approach. Now the mark of the true flaming jackass is his inability to learn from experience, direct or vicarious. I for one am not going to laugh at poor old out-of-date Calvin Rustrum, because he could go out tomorrow with the same gear and techniques he's used for fifty years, head off in the bush of Upper Canada, and spend a winter without missing a meal and spend it comfortably to boot. If Rustrum's thorough knowledge and competency in cold weather humbles you a bit, then read further and really get your arrogance crushed. Take a whack at Vilhjalmur Stefansson's *The Friendly Arctic, Arctic Manual,* and *My Life With the Eskimo.* Read some of the ethnological papers and monographs from the University of Alaska, or Richard Nelson's *Hunters of the Northern Forest* and *Hunters of the Northern Ice.* Get a feeling for how it's done by people who do it all the time. Stefansson in particular writes with an authority (and a background) that's simply overwhelming.

Back to lunch. Take the break. Take the "mug-up" if you can. Park your duff on your pack or your scrap of Ensolite, pull on your big parka, and relax. Chew up a tin of tuna fish in oil, some Triscuits and whatever else pleases you. Swill down all the hot margarined tea you can get. And look at that wonderful white world around you. You're warm, well-fed, well rested. You're completely at home in the toughest environment civilized man has to contend with—or so he thinks. You know better. My, my, isn't all that silence pretty? □

SNOWSHOES

It may strike you as strange that a veteran cross-country ski instructor and long-time propagandizer of that sport should talk about winter travel in terms of snowshoes. It struck **me** as strange for a while. Skinny skis are fun—even the fat skinny skis called "touring skis". It's easy to develop some facility with them, too. But skis are limited by terrain and snow conditions. Snowshoes are for going places: uphills, up steep ravines, through brush, on crust, in that heavy, sticky stuff called "mashed potato snow". If you can walk, you can snowshoe. Despite what a lot of us have said in the past, that isn't true about ski touring.

Be forewarned. Choosing a snowshoe is a process as burdened with mystique as choosing a packframe. Snowshoe vendors may be divided, like Caesar's Gaul, into three groups. The first group is inhabited by the merchant who has a few pairs of shoes tucked into a remote corner, and who unceremoniously plops them down in front of you with a demand for fifty dollars and bids you goodbye. He doesn't know what he's selling and you don't know what you're buying.

The second group of merchants is typified by the bright-eyed, bushy-tailed winter peakbagger who tells you that while he has a selection of snowshoes, **this** is the only one to have. He's an expert; he knows. Problem is, he knows what works for him in rather advanced situations, and he's probably not even considered that your interests may not be his.

The third breed of merchant begins by asking about what you plan to be doing with these gormless-looking oversized tennis racquets, and takes it from there. Well, let's begin here by asking about your plans. Short day hikes with minimum gear? Longer day hikes in more remote country? Peakbagging with a heavy load, either by the day or overnighting? How about the terrain you'll be in? Gentle, rolling country? Bush, spiky and thorny, or pretty much open? Steep hillsides and gulleys? How about the typical snowfall pattern in your favorite area? Not too much snow? Lots of snow that tends to remain fairly loose? Lots of snow, but characterized by a freeze and thaw cycle (typified by the Northeast) that gives

49

you powder one day, breakable crust a day later, boiler plate the next day, slush two days later, and then another snowfall?

All of these factors have a bearing on snowshoe selection. As you can probably guess from looking at the list of questions, no one snowshoe will do everything well. Several models are highly specialized, so much so that the range of their use is almost nil.

Let's look at some basic snowshoe types for a few pages. Again, we can divide them into three main varieties: open country snowshoes, general purpose snowshoes, and climbing snowshoes.

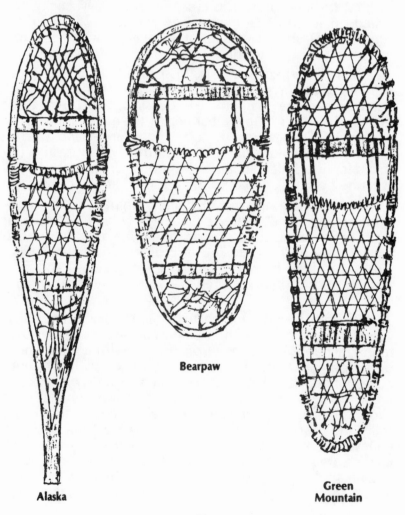

Bearpaw

Alaska

Green
Mountain

The open country snowshoe is what most people think of when the word "snowshoe" is mentioned. It's a tall (5 to 6 feet), narrow (10 to 12 inches) shoe with a strongly upcurved tip and a long tail, and it would look right at home on the wall of Sergeant Preston of the Yukon's cabin. In fact, one of its common names is "Yukon Style" or some such handle. "Cross-country" and "Michigan" are other common designations.

Think of them as short skis. They have a lot of surface area to ensure floatation on deep, soft snow, and that upswept tip enables you to almost jog along without burying the tips of the shoes. The long tail keeps the shoes pointed in a straight line, and reduces the amount of snow-carrying area in the rear of the shoe, so that it's easy to control and use. If you plan to be tramping around relatively open terrain and not get involved in too much brush-scrambling, sidehilling and climbing, there is nothing better. A good snowshoer on the right kind of snow can almost skate on them, and you can even slide a little down hills. They are deservedly popular in places like Michigan and Minnesota, they're what you're offered in most of Canada if you ask for "snowshoes" (or *racquettes* in Quebec), and they're abominable for peakbagging or hill-and-gully scrambling. They tend to turn crosswise on side hills; they're difficult to manage in the puckerbush; the toe is so long and so upswept that steep climbing, which requires a few special techniques, is a travesty.

At the other extreme is the climbing shoe. Most folks don't call them that, but one look at the dour, squat little beasts will tell you what they're used for. Typically they're short, wide for their length, flat, tailess, and short-toed. A 28-inch long snowshoe that's 13 inches wide is handy in tight quarters. Less obvious to the novice is the usefulness of the short, flat toe. The skilled webfooter uses that stubby toe as a climbing aid on steep, scrambly terrain. Just swing the leg and kick that snowshoe toe straight into the snow and stand on it. It works. (Well, it works if the snow is reasonably compacted. If the snow's soft, it's more than useless, and if the snow is hard and deeply crusted, you bounce.)

The climbing shoe has distince advantages on steep terrain, but unless you plan to do a lot of climbing, you'd be best advised to consider its shortcomings. The flat toe digs in on descents—and sometimes on a level trail. The fat after-body flips a lot of snow up on your legs and backside, and some wider models, the 14-and-15-inches, are too wide to faill comfortably in normal walking unless you're long-legged. Nothing is quite as disconcerting as picking up a snowshoe and finding that the other one is firmly planted on top of it.

If you've gotten the impression that I'm not exactly in love with the standard issue climbing shoe, which masquerades as "bearpaw, G.I. bearpaw, or modified bearpaw", you're right. For a pure climbing shoe, I prefer a short, narrow, upswept toe shoe. The classic design of this type is the Green Mountain Bearpaw, by Vermont Tubbs, a 36-inch long, 10-inch wide shoe with an upturned toe. While this was conceived as a general-purpose snowshoe, it works well in steep country. It's difficult to "kick in" the toe, of course, but it's narrow enough to turn sideways and kick in edgewise. Like most bearpaws (best described as tailless shoes), it kicks up a lot of snow on the back of your legs, but it's long enough to track well and narrow enough to be easy walking for almost anybody.

I have a particular favorite for steep terrain—a very small, aluminum-framed shoe by Sherpa that resembles a short Green Mountain Bearpaw. It's very light, very easily managed in crowded conditions, works on trails well due to a generously upturned toe, is narrow enough (and short enough) to edge easily, and has an absolutely marvelous binding system. Sherpa calls it the "Lightfoot", and you'd have to pry mine off my cold, stiff feet to get them from me if I couldn't get another pair. I'm aware that the size is a whole lot smaller than the tables recommended for my all-up weight; in fact, they're smaller than the experts would recommend for ol' HNR stripped of pack, clothing and even beard. But they work.

Which brings up a point that has to be dealt with sooner or later—that of snowshoe size. Most people get snowshoes that are far too big for them to handle comfortably. With the exception of the long, skinny trail shoes, where longer is definitely better, many snowshoers are clumping around with something that could be replaced by any convenient garbage pail top with no loss in mobility. The argument behind the tables of sizes you'll see in most outfitter's catalogs is that the appropriately-sized shoe is necessary to keep you from sinking out of sight in deep snow. You won't vanish if you use a smaller snowshoe. You won't even have to be saved by the fact that your legs grow together somewhere due south of your waist. Snow is a plastic medium. After it's sat awhile and been and rolled by the breeze, it consolidates. It gets firmer. True, there is powder snow hip deep on a bull elk in some areas of the West on which nothing but card tables on each trotter will keep you afloat—but even that is relatively short-lived. In the East and Midweat? Forget it! Get a pair of snowshoes that's small enough to manage comfortably and easily, and go on the assumption that five percent of the time the snow will be too fluffy and unconsolidated for really easy travel. I don't know about you, but I'm just lazy enough to opt for ease and convenience 95 percent of the time and hard work 5 percent of the time rather than the reverse!

Somewhere between those ridges of lofty purpose, the climbing shoe and the trail shoe, is the humble valley of general purpose snowshoes. And to extend the metaphor, like most valleys it's broad and fertile and has grown a diverse crop.

The general-purpose snowshoes are most frequently shoes with tails, the Green Mountain Bearpaw being a notable exception. In general design, they're fatter than a trailshoe but leaner than a bearpaw. They have upturned tips (often very shallow curves), and they have short to medium length tails. Unlike the bearpaw and its brothers, they tend to taper sharply behind the binding area, and are generally widest before the master cord. This reduces the tendency to step on your own snowshoe a bit.

As you've begun to notice, a snowshoe isn't something slapped together by somebody with a whim of iron. The proportions and elements of its design have been fixed by a few hundred years of terribly pragmatic people. The tail on a snowshoe isn't there for good looks. It's there to help the shoe track, to reduce snow load and snow kickback on your legs, and to reduce drag. The after part of the shoe is contoured in such a way that the toe fits nicely alongside it for easy walking. The length of the toe is a function of the overall length of the shoe and of the placement of the master cord. Too long a toe results in a shoe whose tail won't drop when you're moving along. Not only does this cause the toe to dig in, but it places heavy load on the muscles that run along the skins. This brings on what my *Habitant* kin call *mal de racquette,* and it makes shin splints feel as pleasant as a sauna and a cold ale after a good winter hike.

You can almost take for granted that any snowshoe you'll pick up respects these classical proportions. It's simply a question of determining what set of proportions will best do the job. If you're in country where the trail shoe reigns supreme, there's no problem. In most terrain, you have to think about it, though—and that's where some assessment of your desires comes into play. If you want a pleasant, low-key ramble in moderate terrain, you'll probably look toward the longer, leaner general purpose shoe. That same pleasant, low-key ramble in more hilly terrain might dictate a shorter, stouter shoe with a stubby tail rather than a long tail. I would never recommend a climbing shoe as a first or only pair of snowshoes—with one exception. A lot of folks like to ski tour as far into the puckerbush and as high up a mountain as they can easily manage, and then don their webbed feet for the final leg of the journey. If that's your bag, then the climbing shoe, suitably tricked out, is your shoe.

If I had to live with one snowshoe type for all uses in the Northeast—as snowshoes aren't cheap, this isn't a bad idea—it would be a stubby-tailed shoe with a relatively slim after-body, and a short but slightly upturned toe. While this type is often erroneously called a "modified bearpaw," we Upstaters know it as a Westover. The design was developed by Floyd Westover of the small settlement of Meco, close by Johnstown, New York, and a genuine Westover-built Westover shoe is to the York State snowshoer as a Eugene Jensen cedar stripper is to the canoe racer. It's the real thing. Most snowshoe builders never saw wood as good as Floyd Westover discarded, and those terribly slim, fragil-looking frames were springy and light and tough beyond compare. A damn fool could break one. Snowshoes aren't bridges, after all. And they don't take kindly to being kicked against rocks. But with normal use and some care, a good snowshoe will last a lifetime.

All this bring up some questions. What's "normal use"? How much care is "some care"? And what's a "good" snowshoe?

Let's answer the last question first. Chances are that the snowshoes you'll be looking at will be wood-framed rather than aluminum-framed. This isn't intended to put down the aluminum snowshoe. The ones I've used (Sherpa, Early Winters, and Black Forest) are good. Nevertheless, they are primarily mountaineering shoes rather than truckin' around shoes, and are intended for tough going in tough country. You probably won't need them. If you do, you'll know it without me telling you. The heart of a traditional wood-framed shoe is obviously the wood. There is one wood for snowshoe frames—white ash. Surprisingly enough, dense-grained North Country white ash, which conventional woodworking wisdom would consider most desirable, is too dense and too brittle. The ideal log is from south slope-grown trees that shows 10 to 15 annual rings per inch. Less than that results in an easily abraded frame that lacks strength; more results in brittleness and excessive weight. A good frame should show a reasonably open grain, and the grain should be straight. Grain that runs out to the edge is unacceptable, period.

It's common practice in better shoes to lean out the wood at the very tip to reduce internal stresses after forming and to make the shoe "hang" better. This, of course, makes the shoe more prone to damage if you're into rooting rocks around with it, but it is not a sign of weakness unless the job has been botched badly and the shoe has been left overfine. Check to see that any holes drilled in the frame are well centered and not spotted so that they become built-in stress risers. Check also that the crosspieces are properly placed and that the frame has been inletted properly to accept it. The life of the shoe shouldn't be hanging on a mere thread of wood at those points.

Note also if the master cord is square to the shoe. A master cord that's skeewoogy means that one shoe wants to track a few compass points off. It may be only a minor irrita-tion, but who needs even a minor irritation? I don't. You don't. Not at what snowshoes are selling for today, we don't!

There isn't much you can do to evaluate the lacing except to check that it's snug and that no laces are skived halfway through or have unusually fine spots in an otherwise stout-looking strand. Fine lacing in and of itself is no problem. Many styles are traditionally laced in the toe with fine rawhide, and the body lacing of Canadian shoes, particularly the Indian-made ones, is traditionally of finely cut hide.

The same criteria apply to neoprene-coated nylon lac-ing, with a couple of exceptions. Rawhide laces should be tight. Hide is laced wet, and on drying, the hide shrinks. After drying, the shoes are dipped in varnish to protect both the frames and the laces. Neoprene/nylon laces will not be as tight as hide. The material, however, will not stretch and sag when wet, so this doesn't matter. A well-laced neoprene/nylon shoe will have a springy feeling, but it will not be as stiff as hide. As long as it's firm, it should be acceptable. In those places where the frame is wrapped several times, make certain that the laces are well-fixed. Neoprene/nylon is a miserable material to work with. It has no elasticity to speak of, and it is most unkind to the operator's hands. No, it's neither toxic nor a cause of contact dermatitis; it's simply like conducting a day-long taffy pull with garnet paper taffy! It's a whole lot easier to make a mistake with neoprene/nylon. So look before you buy. You don't have to be fanatical about it. The folks who build snowshoes are pretty much dedicated to righteous craftmanship. They'd better be—it's not a business that would attract anybody who was dedicated solely to massive capital gains and enamoured of highly efficient manufacturing techniques.

Now about that weasel-worded phrase, "some care." Well, anything made of wood that's exposed to the elements requires some affectionate fussing. And if you can tell a hawk from a handsaw, you know that rawhide will stretch and sag if it gets wet. Both wood and rawhide loathe excessive heat and both dote on a good flexible exterior grade polyurethane varnish. I reckon your brand is as good as mine. I've used Varathane a lot for snowshoes and canoe paddles, which works well. Something else might be better, but I'm happy with it. (And the discount house in town carries it!)

A snowshoe bare of varnish is unhappy—and one day spent romping around on corn snow or breakable crust will strip a snowshoe of a lot of varnish. If you must dry the laces in the field for the next day's trek because they've sagged, don't expose them to more heat than your hand can take. If you **hold** the snowshoes while you're drying them, you'll rarely cook your laces. When you get home, air-dry the shoes, sand off any raggedy edges, and get out the brush and varnish. Thin out the first coat, and put on the second straight from the can. If you have the time, do three coats: one thin, the next less thin, and the last "straight."

Neoprene/nylon laces are impervious to moisture, so you needn't do anything with them. They can break, as can hide, and they're easier to repair than hide in the field because you don't have to soften them first. The frames still need their regular varnishing. Don't worry about the laces. You can varnish right over the laces passed around the frame with impunity. It'll simply peel off in time.

Minor repairs of neoprene/nylon laces are straightforward and obvious. Hide is trickier. It's naturally worked wet which means the repair piece is wet and soft and the laces that need repair are wet and soft as well. The first part is easy: toss the repair piece into a pot of water. The second part may require some tinkering. I do it this way. I scrape the varnish off the hide to be repaired, giving myself as much of a piece to work with as I can get. Work both broken ends back to the frame if you can. I like to scrape with a jackknife, scraping toward me with the blade angled away from me (or vice versa if you dislike working toward yourself with a knife). Next, I steam the strands of hide with a teakettle to start the softening process. Then I lay the shoe across a shallow pan filled with water and wrap the offending strands only with wet cloth, one end of which reposes soddenly in the pan. When the hide is soft, cut slits in the ends of both broken strands. Cut in the center of the strand, and leave yourself a ¼-inch of uncut lace at the end.

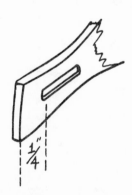

If the lace has stretched badly and thinned, or if it shows sings of incipient failure, cut it back to where it's sound before you slit it.

Now take your repair piece, cut a slit in one and like the two you just cut in the broken strands. Poke the end of the broken strand through the slit in the repair piece, and then poke the free end of the repair piece through the slit in the broken strand. The operation looks like this:

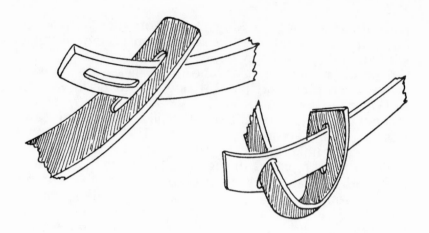

Pull the pieces snugly together. Do it **gently;** wet hide isn't exactly 304L stainless steel.

Now poke the free end of the repair piece through the slit in the other broken lace, draw up gently (remember, the hide will shrink when dry) and take a quick half-hitch to secure it. **Before** you cut off the excess lace, cut a diagonal slit in the free end just past the knot. Cut halfway through or a bit beyond, like so:

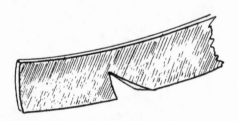

Then go out on the lace a half-inch or so beyond the slit and cut it off. The purpose of the slit is to form a nifty little lock for the half-hitch sould the lace be softened inadvertently in use. Varnish the repair twice after it's dried, and you're set to go. While you have the varnish out, you might as well give both shoes a treat, and do them completely. They'll love you for it.

Some folks say that too much varnish makes the shoes slippery on crust. It probably does, but if the crust is thick, you'll be wearing crampons (metal spikes on a frame that attaches to your boots, of which more later) and won't need snowshoes. If the crust is thin, you'll be using creepers on your snowshoes. We'll talk about them later, too.

Right now, let's talk about bindings, the things that unite your feet and your snowshoes. Most webfooters are fanatical boosters of one type of binding over all others, and I'm no exception. What I like shouldn't influence you in this instance. When I tell you about hypothermia and its causes, symptoms and treatment, you'd better listen. When I tell you about insulation or shelter or a lot of other things, pay attention. I'll be careful to note a personal preference (a whim, if you will), as just that, which means "make up your own mind."

A binding must do certain things reliably and easily. It must be adjustable with a minimum of fussing. It must keep the ball of your foot positioned over the master cord without slipping. It must keep your foot aligned properly on the snowshoe without letting your heel schwobble laterally, even on side hills. It must be dependable, and it must maintain its configuration and size regardless of weather. Finally, it must do all these things without being drawn up so tightly that it impedes circulation in your feet.

Each of the three major styles of binding acts in the same way. A toepiece of some sort, attached to the master cord, positions the toe properly and keeps the boot from sliding forward or sideways, and a heelpiece, attached either to the toepiece or to the master cord, maintains tension on the boot and keeps it in the toepiece. That's all there is to it. Now let's look at some specific binding types.

The commonest and simplest is a pattern called the "H" binding. The toepiece is formed by a long strap with a buckle on one end and a rectangular piece of leather (or neoprene/nylon) with four slits in it, like so.

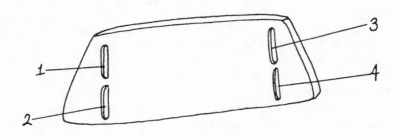

The toepiece is formed by passing the strap down through (1), around the master cord and up through (2). The strap then goes across, down through (3), around the master cord, and up through (4), where it can now be buckled. Some folks prefer to cross-lace the strap (i.e., go from [2] to [4] and then to [3]); I don't. Neither cross-lacers nor straight-lacers have any good reasons for their choices, so do whatever comes easier to hand.

Heel location is provided by two long straps. One end of each is looped, woven, or buckled around the master cord. They're buckled together on one side of the heel after the longer one is passed around behind the boot. To complete the rig, an instep strap is secured to the heel straps, usually by slits in the instep strap through which the heel strap is passed. The instep strap passes under the boot and buckles on top of the instep.

The "H" is light, simple, easily repaired or jury-rigged in the field, and inexpensive. It's sloppy fore-and-aft, although a piece of parachute cord between the toepiece and the instep helps somewhat, and it's sloppy laterally unless the heel straps are positioned as close to the frame as possible on the master cord. In use, the toe strap stays put; once adjusted, it shouldn't need to be unbuckled. The instep strap and the heel strap are unbuckled with each use. The leather "H" stretches too much to be a truly pleasant binding; I prefer the neoprene/nylon.

Another popular unit is the Howe binding and innumerable modifications of same. The genuine Howe, as made in leather by Vermont Tubbs, is a complicated rig, but most pleasant to use. Figuring out how to put one together with just the pieces is an interesting exercise in futility; so I'll tell you how to do it. In the process, you should get a good notion of why the Howe works well.

When you unwrap the bag containing a Howe binding, you'll be greeted by two sets of the following: 2 straps about 11 inches long with buckles on one end and longitudinal slits on the other end. These mount close to the frame on the master cord. Loop the slit end around the cord, push the buckle through it, and draw up tight. So much for that. Next you'll find 2 straps about 26 inches long, with buckles on one end and perforations like belt holes running in more or less orderly fashion on the other end. These serve as toe strap and instep strap. Next you'll find a piece of leather about 2⅜ inches wide and 11 inches long, with five slits paralleling each side. Four sets are pretty much equidistant; the fifth set is a bit further aft. The oddball slits are for the instep strap, but don't sweat that now.

Next you'll find another 2⅜-inch wide piece about 13 inches long with a long strap (25 inches if you're curious) riveted on the middle at the center of the wide strap. It's the heel piece.

As the old MG repair manual used to state, "henceforth the operation is straightforward." We've already attached the forward parts of the side hitches to the master cord. After this, it's easy to buckle the big heel strap to the side hitches, and it's easy to thread one of the long straps through one of those oddball slits in the toe strap, through the slits in one side of the heel piece (thread from the inside to the outside and then to the inside), under where the boot instep would be, up through the other side of the heel strap, and back to the toe strap. So far so good.

Now we have to figure out how to attach the toe piece to the master cord of the snowshoe. This is guaranteed to drive you up a wall—but you only have to do it once if the binding's of neoprene, and you'll have to tinker it a little from time to time if it's leather to accommodate a tendency to stretch.

Put the snowshoe on your lap and take a minute to stroke it affectionately. Whether of warm wood or cold aluminum, it's a true and useful tool for transportation, and it deserves some affection and respect. Now, count the laces running from the master cord back to the tail that comes up to the toe opening. Not counting the laces that run back from the corners of the toe opening, you'll either find two or three. Three's easier to handle, but two's okay. Put your boot in the binding and adjust the heel straps so that the ball of your foot will be centered over the master cord. Now you can tell which one of those four sets of inscrutable die-cut slots is the right one to use! Fasten the instep strap in place, and run the toepiece over the toe of the boot and then between the boot and the master cord. Chances are that either the first or second set of slots will fall nicely in line with the laces. If it doesn't exactly, don't worry. Typically, you'll start by threading the toe strap through the slot next to the instep strap, and down through old #1 left slot, around the snowshoe lace, back up through old #1 left, across to the right side of #1, and down, around the other snowshoe lace, back up through #1 right, and up through the slot opposite where you started. This way, you've "locked" that toepiece down and given it some stability. You want it to flex easily fore-and aft—but not laterally.

This same approach works for the various Howe-type bindings in leather or in neoprene. I should point out that the serious snowshoer's standard binding is a modified Howe built meticulously and durably in neoprene by an expatriate New Hampshireman named Bruce Beck, who also builds crampon straps that have been to every major summit in the world.

The Howe is beloved of snowshoers because it isn't sloppy, and it won't let your toe "kick through" the binding on a steep descent or a steep, step-kicking ascent as will the old H-pattern. The Howe also doesn't have to be really snug at any place, which makes it excellent for use with shoepacs or mukluks, where a binding that has to be really snug can be most detrimental to your comfort and, in time, your circulation.

As might be expected, new concepts in snowshoes, as evidenced in the Sherpa, Early Winters and Black Forest aluminum shoes, have brought about new binding concepts or refinements of old ones. That they work is indisputable; that they're always comfortable with shoepacs is open to some debate. As I've said, I use a little pair of Sherpas for climbing, and they function beautifully. But I can't say I find the binding comfortable except when I'm wearing my old Mouse boots. I haven't used the other shoes enough to have any strong feelings about binding comfort. Of course, if it was a real hassle, I could adapt a Howe to work on any of them. That I haven't simply indicates that I may be just enough of a woodchuck to have an irrational prejudice for the ways in which I've always done things, regardless of their merits.

I shouldn't close this chapter without a few words on snowshoeing technique. I hadn't planned on it, figuring that walking on snowshoes is just like any other kind of walking, but the more I think of it, the more some words on technique are necessary.

To begin with, you can't walk naturally on snowshoes that are too wide for you. If you're in easy terrain and plan to lope along on Yukons, this is no trouble. But if you're doing hill and dale stuff, particularly with a heavy pack (and a winter pack is always heavier for the same trip than a summer pack), an overly wide snowshoe can do a number on your hip joints. I don't care what the books say, friend; get as narrow a shoe as you can possible squeak by with.

Walking on webs is easy. Just walk. For most climbing at reasonable angles, just climb straight up. In steeper terrain, I prefer to traverse. With small shoes, I can traverse a path that's level by placing one shoe almost directly in front of the other. Larger shoes necessitate a traverse in which the trail broken by one foot is higher than the other, leaving something fit to be followed by that mythical animal called the sidehill gouge, who always traverses hills and has, in consequence, developed long legs on one side and short ones on the other. (Which also means that there must be clockwise and counterclockwise gouges, and that a clockwise gouge would topple down the mountin if he ran in a counter-clockwise direction, but that's enough of that!) Very steep, short sections can be attacked by kicking steps, a maneuver which requires a short-toed but not necessarily a straight-toed shoe. To kick a step, swing your leg back, then forward, driving the toe of the shoe (and your boot) about 12 to 18 inches into the snow. Climb the snowshoe as if it were a step of a ladder, and kick in the other one. Obviously the snow can't be too hard for this maneuver; neither can it be too soft. And if the stretch you have to kick steps into is a long one, the chances are that you're flirting with an avalanche hazard. Find another route—even in the East. Avalanches occur in the Adirondacks and Whites too. They may not be as large or as spectacular, but they can be just as deadly. The avalanche control experts in the Rockies estimate that a 20 foot wide slide that takes only a **six-inch** snow depth with it can bury a climber or a skier in 100 feet. Westerners, especially those who wander the Rockies, the Sierras and the Wasatch, are pretty watchful and well informed. Easterners in general and Easterners who go West are best advised to do some boondocking with somebody who's able to point out the hazards. No book can do it for you.

A lot of snowshoe travelers simply walk along; others, and I'm one of them, prefer some sort of balance device, particularly in steeper terrain. The most convenient is a pair of ski poles, sturdy ones. The steep terrain webfooter may need an ice axe with a snow basket pulled over the shaft at the pick end. I have to concede a fondness for the ice axe. Like a snowshoe, it's a completely functional, and therefore, a completely beautiful tool. And it's not without its uses even in the gentle hills that I roam around! But I suspect that the ski poles work better for low-country ramblers. The old GI ones with the huge baskets and heavy shafts are probably the best obtainable for the purpose. □

FROM THE SKIN OUT

Clothing for the summer hiker can be seemingly unimportant, but clothing is obviously of supreme importance to the winter hiker. Yet short hikes and day trips are possible with what you can find in your closet, as we've already seen. If you plan to go further, or not be limited to easy trips in mellow weather, your clothing will begin to take on a specialized—and I fear somewhat costly—aspect.

Let's start from the inside out with clothing. At risk of boring you, I'll be talking again and again about some basic items and some basic ideas. One of these ideas is that the winter trekker should carry duplicate clothing except for parkas. On a long trip, the notion has value. On a short trip or a day's ramble, it's not necessary. Some items should be duplicated even on a long day trip, though. We'll mention these as we go along.

Socks

Let's start with the feet—or more specifically, what's under your boots. Wool is the rule. While a lot of folks will debate this a bit, I opt for two pairs of ragg wool socks of a sufficient length to keep the tops of the boots from eating holes in your calves. This isn't a problem if your calves are full. I'm definitely spindleshanked, and my boots do terrible things to my legs. Woolen socks, of course, are superfluous if you happen to have a pair of Mouse boots. Socks should be changed out whenever they get damp—again, the exception is the Mouse boot—and this requires extras. On a multi-day trip, you may wind up carrying fresh socks for every day, because you can't reliably dry them. I have taken boot socks (the drier of the two pair) into my sleeping bag with me, which dries them nicely, but for long trips this could result in adding more moisture to the bag's insulation, which is unacceptable. If you're allergic to wool, Orlon is the only really useful alternative. Don't be tempted by things like down socks. They squash down to wool sock thickness in use, and they're impossible to dry in the field. I'm tempted, nevertheless, to put together *Polarguard* socks and try them this winter—just for the hell of it. That makes sense, at any rate.

Socks: Take two spare pairs on day hikes, more for longer journeys.

Underwear

Underwear is not a subject to be taken lightly, believe me. It has to be warm, comfortable, and ventilatable. And you'd best be fond of your underwear; because if you're like most winter hikers, you'll live in your underwear day and night.

To begin with, avoid **any** underwear that you can't ventilate. Remember—insulation layers are effective only when they're dry, and perspiration is the commonest way they'll get wet in winter.

The easiest way to achieve ventilatable underwear is to begin with a fishnet shirt and fishnet long johns of wool or wool and polyester or cotton and polyester. This fishnet is remarkable stuff. It's thick enough to provide a good insulation layer if you're buttoned up and battened down around camp, but being nothing more than a bunch of holes held together by string, it ventilates with incredible ease when you unbutton.

Depending on the weather and the nature of your trip, you may want to wear an insulating layer of underwear over the fishnet. Try to avoid an undershirt (an over-undershirt??) that you can't ventilate. The typical crew-neck undershirt will turn your fishnet into an insulating layer rather than a layer that does double duty. You can beat the bushes for a GI undershirt or get a Duofold "River Driver's Shirt," both of which have buttons at the neck. Another alternative is an old wool shirt. You know the kind—sleeves that are more hole than cloth, and a collar frayed beyond repair. Well, remove the sleeves completely. Don't cut them off short—remove them from where they're set in. Remove the collar too, if you choose. And whatta ya got? A wool vest with buttons up the front—or a wool over-under shirt that's warm when you want warmth and ventilatable when you get too warm. There's another virtue, too. It not only costs you nothing, it actually makes useful a useless garment. I'm enough of a skinflint—anybody with a large family has got to be—to enjoy that double saving.

Ventilation isn't as critical from the waist down, but is more difficult to achieve. About all you can do is unzip or unbutton your fly if you wear a belt. I wear suspenders, so I can loosen the little snugger tabs on my GI pants and ventilate nicely. But I rarely need to. I'm skinny and like to think of myself as slender, but 6'3" and 155 pounds is a travesty of "slender." Willowy? Lean? No. Skinny's the word. And my pipecleaner-width shanks are happy with a generous amount of insulation. Yours will be too, in all probability. Keep that warm blood warm en route to your feet and your toes will love you for it.

If you don't like ankle-length woolies, you could use another old woodchuck's trick to advantage. Your winter pants are loose, right? This means that you can probably fit another pair of pants under them. Here's the place for those threadbare wool and polyester pants in the closet! Chop 'em off above the knees, amputate the pockets, and you have cheap, serviceable balbriggan drawers in five minutes. Me? I just pull on a pair of wool and polyester blend long johns over the fishnet long johns and go on the assumption that my legs can never get too warm.

Take a back-up set of underwear for an overnight. A spare fishnet top is useful on a day trip. Treat a hard day trip like an overnight.

Pants

Wool or a wool blend, loose and roomy, with no cuffs, in a nutshell. I'd add a few desirable fillips. Pants pockets on a winter hike are among the truly useless trappings of civilization, right up there with television game shows. Everything falls out of pockets except snow, which finds every opening in your armor with remarkable accuracy. Pull out the linings and sew the little devils shut, unless you have the patience to set zippers in them or sew flaps over them that you can close with Velcro.

As I've said, I like suspenders in wintertime, because they afford a means of ventilating an otherwise inaccessible region of one's anatomy. To be able to do this, you need pants that fit loosely around the middle. However, loose pants aren't always a joy and a treasure. There are times when you want to button up snugly. You could wear a belt, but it's easier to sew two sets of mini-belts onto your pants. Half-inch nylon tape works just fine. We'll do one side to show you how. You'll need sixteen inches of nylon tape and two Tabler buckles (the shoulder strap adjusters on your daypack are probably Tabler buckles, and chances are that your local backpacking shop has them or something like them). If not, your hardware shop may. Sew one end of a five inch long piece of tape to your

67

pants where the belt would normally go, and sew it in such a way that the loose end reaches to your side. Be generous with your stitching. Use a half-inch of the tape, and sew it down in a box and cross pattern, like this:

Now, run a piece of tape through the anchor end of the buckle, turn it back about an inch, and sew the two pieces of tape together with a box and cross, like this:

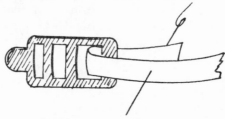

Sew this piece on to the waistband of the pants so that the free end of the tape just engages the buckle. This way, the buckle and strap aren't dangling loose. The system is already threaded if you need to snug up on a cold day, and you have about four inches of "travel" on each side that you can use to snug up your loose, comfortable pants.

Oh, yes. I forgot. Go do the same thing to the other side of your pants. Symmetry is beautiful!

Other alterations are possible. A double seat is a thing of beauty and a joy forever—and isn't easy to sew. Somebody with some smarts around a sewing machine can do it, but for those of you who march in the first ranks of the Klutz Brigade next to me, it's a spiteful job. However, even I can take the discarded legs of an old pair of wool pants—maybe the ones you cut off for those do-it-yourself balbriggans—and double the front of the pants legs down to the knees. Some folks even go so far as to slit the outside seam of the pants legs up a foot or so from where the cuffs would be if you were wearing cuffs—which you're not—and install zippers so they can shinny out of their pants in camp without having to take off their boots. I don't do it, but my admiration for such ingenuity is exceeded only by my admiration for anybody who has the courage to wander around camp clad only in boots and fishnet long johns!

Some folks take extra pants for an overnight. I will in Spring, when the snow is wet and some streams may be open. For a long trip, I'd take extra pants.

Shirts 'N' Such

Insulation for your upper body is almost inevitably a shirt. I have nothing against sweaters, and will often carry a wool turtleneck for campwear. But most sweaters are pullovers, and pullovers, even with V-necks, don't provide enough ventilation. You're better off with a light shirt and a heavier shirt in cold going. It's easy to find a good and reasonably inexpensive heavy wool shirt. The light woolens have become fashion items, and correspondingly costly. Let me tell you, friend. It will be a cold day in the North Country before you'll find ol' Harry wearing a forty-dollar Pendleton on a winter trip! In fact, I'd make this generalization: If it's so cold out that you **need** two shirts plus undershirt and mountain parka to keep warm while you're hiking with a full pack, it's probably too cold to have an enjoyable trip. Sure, it's fine to talk about -30°F nights to your friends, but a -30°F night is easier to cope with than the -15°F day that preceded it and that will follow it. When you've done it enough to have routinized your operations, and you both know and trust your gear from experience, then you'll find that there's a magic about very cold weather. But until you have your kit together, forget it. You're not going out there to prove something. You're going out there to recreate yourself in a world that's so uncluttered, so clean, and so quiet that you'll have trouble believing it.

There's nothing complicated or tricky about a heavy wool shirt. Make sure it's roomy enough over your underwear, and long enough in the shirttail to stay put when you want it to stay put. I'd also suggest that you make certain that the buttons are well and truly secured. I use 20 pound test braided nylon casting line on mine!

I don't see a need for a back-up shirt on a day trip, even a hard one. On a long trip, a back-up shirt might well be in order.

Headgear

Headgear is so important to the winter outdoorsperson that it deserves a separate chapter. The old bush ranger's adage, "When your feet are cold, put your hat on," is both absolutely true and widely ignored by many tyros.

If you'll hearken back to our earlier chats about how cold affects us and about insulation, you'll remember that the body does not throttle down the flow of warm, oxygen-rich blood to the head and the torso. You've also, in all probability, either had or witnessed a scalp laceration. You bleed like a stuck pig! Your scalp, nape, and throat are unusually well-endowed with arteries, veins and capillaries; so well so that fifteen percent of your body's heat is lost through your scalp in a situation where all parts of your body are at or close to normal temperature. In severe weather, that figure can go up to over thirty percent. This means that your head must be well protected. This means also that whatever headgear you use must be sufficiently flexible to permit gradations in ventilation—*even if it means carrying two hats.* Come to think of it, that's not too outlandish an idea. I do it all the time!

Hats are wool, Orlon or bulky nylon, or a combination of the above. I prefer wool, but some people who can wear woolen mittens, socks, long johns and shirts can't abide wool hats. Fortunately, Orlon hats are widely available, and the material is the next best thing to wool. I'll tell you what I wear and why. Alter my system as you see fit.

I wear my hair in what could be called a "communications industry shag"—in other words, moderately long. In winter, it's cut much shorter. Sure, the hair is insulation, but it's uncontrolled insulation. A sweaty, wet mop at the back of my head will chill me to the bone in no time—and it doesn't have to be a bitterly cold day for that to happen. So, I start with moderately short hair. Over that goes the basic hat, a woolen Balaclava that once was orange but now faintly resembles a middle-aged school bus. A Balaclava is a hat that unrolls to protect your cheeks and chin, and snuggles around your neck. Mine is fairly loosely woven, so it requires protection against wind penetration on a blustery day. I can wear it above my ears, over my ears, over my ears and nape, over ears, nape and forehead, or all the way down. It's an admirable garment and a tried and true trail companion of many years.

My other hat is a lightweight wool job that's long enough to pull down over the nape of my neck. It's not very thick—scarcely thicker than a T-shirt—but it works well in mild weather and it's my constant companion at night. Yes, I wear a nightcap on a winter trip—and sometimes on a summer trip. Sometimes at home, too!

There's also a third "hat." Like the first two, absolutely indispensible. It's the hood on my mountain parka. It protects the insulation layer of my hat from wind losses and keeps the hat dry in a rain or a snowfall. It protects my face from wind and blowing snow. We'll talk more about parkas in a minute, but for the nonce, know that good, deep parka hood is the glue that holds your head's insulation together—and your head's insulation holds **you** together!

Mountain Parkas

So far, the gear we've talked about—even boots—can be improvised or purchased inexpensively. Chances are good that you have most of it around the house. However, if you've been mostly a three-season wilderness roamer, you probably don't have a mountain parka. You'll need the versatile protection that this big shell garment provides—and you won't get that kind of protection from a light 2.2 oz. nylon taffeta windshell, regardless of how good it may be. The lightweight shell may be all you need for mild weather walks around home. If that's what you're interested in, don't go out and spend the heavy bucks that a mountain parka requires. On the other hand, I live in my parka in winter—and in late fall and early spring, too. Not just on the trail. I wear it to work, to the store, almost everywhere, in fact. A parka's a true universal garment—handsome, functional, tough, windproof and very water-repellent.

The typical mountain parka is a double-shell garment. The exterior shell is usually of a polyester/cotton blend, and the garment is partly lined with either nylon or a lighter weight polyester/cotton. There are some exceptions. You might even say that exceptions are the rule and you wouldn't be far off. Some outer shells are made of either British-made Ventile Cloth, a very tightly woven cotton, or an American fabric called Venture Cloth, which is woven in the same pattern as Ventile and is essentially the equivalent of that almost legendary fabric. Other parkas use a new material called *Gore-Tex*, a waterproof, breathable laminate of nylon and microporous polytetrafluoroethylene that bids fair to be one of the true "miracle fabrics" of contemporary textile engineering. More on *Gore-Tex* later—much more.

The inner linings come in various configurations, the most typical being an upper body lining. At times, the upper arms are lined; at times, the hood is lined. Some parkas are fully lined—arms, hood, upper body and skirt. Needless to say, you get what you pay for. What you're paying for is material and needlework. More material and more sewing is required for a fully-lined parka than for a partly-lined one. Additional material and operator time is required to do a really full, deep hood as opposed to a skimpy one, or to do a full cut across the shoulders instead of a snug one. The benefits aren't immediately perceivable, but the fuller cut means that the garment won't compress your insulation, restrict your movements, and ride up over your backside when you lift your arms above half-mast.

Garment cutting is both an art and a science, and there is always a tradeoff taking place. Virtually all manufacturers of mountain parkas are aware of what could be called "optimum configuration." They're also aware of the fact that to cut an optimum hood and raglan shoulder may leave an extra half-yard of scrap on the cutting table because they can't interlock patterns as well as possible. An additional ten minutes may be required on the table and thirty minutes of needle time. By the time all this (and more) gets to the bottom line, you'll pay up to thirty or forty percent more for a top-of-the-line parka than for a run-of-the-mill one. But remember that the run-of-the-mill one is still a very fine garment!

Here's what to look for in a mountain parka. Go to your friendly local outfitter's with some gear in hand. If you plan to wear the parka over a heavy wool shirt—and you will—bring the wool shirt. Bring a vest, too, because you'll probably be wearing both the shirt and vest around camp, or when you stop to lunch. In general, it's good that your mountain parka can fit over a down or polyester jacket, but unless you're going into some rough country, chances are that you don't need wind protection over a full expedition jacket. If you do, you know it without me telling you. Oh, yes, bring your big, fat Balaclava too.

To begin with, the mountain parka should be long enough to cover your backside with a little to spare. The closure system should be redundant; zipper **and** snaps are virtually universal, and necessary. The flap covering the zipper should be sufficiently wide to exclude drafts and blowing snow, and my preference is for a double-bug zipper that can be opened from the bottom for ventilation if I so choose.

However, you can use the snaps to arrange that—and the double-bug zipper will increase the cost of the parka a bit.

The parka should have a drawcord or some other arrangement around the middle so it can be snugged down to exclude drafts on a windy day, and snugged down to fit on those days when you're not wearing a vest or a light jacket under it. Make sure that the drawcord hits you in a comfortable place. I'm very long waisted, and a lot of cords grab me around the short ribs—hardly no fun at all!

Obviously, the parka should fit comfortably over your wool shirt and vest. "Comfort" you'll have to define for yourself, but there are some functional hints to consider. First and foremost, you don't want a shell garment that's so snug that it compresses your insulation layer even when you stretch your arms in front of you. Further, you should be able to raise your arms over your head with your vest on without either dramatically shortening your sleeves or pulling the jacket up over your backside. Sometimes this means buying a size larger than really looks natty on the street. The alternatives are to make your own from one of the many kits available and "tailor in" the room you need, or spend a lot of pelf for a parka that's cut without regard for scrap loss, like the Synergy Works expedition parka. Bring money. **Lots** of money.

Now to the hood. When the parka's zipped up, is it snug around the neck without inhibiting shoulder and head movement and without causing your sleeves to crawl up to your elbows? Fine. Does the hood fit over your Balaclava without giving you the feeling that your head's in a vise? Good. Can you draw the hood down to a tunnel closure that protects *all* of your face? Good. Can you turn your head with the hood drawn down without burying your face in the hood and blinding yourself? Chances are that you can't, and you'll have to live with it. The Synergy Works parka, again, has a superb hood, and several companies have borrowed the design for their parka hoods, so you'll find a few hoods that you can see out of to the sides. You won't find many. Unless you recut the yoke of the jacket and the sleeves, you won't be able to modify a hood to affect that, either.

Sleeves long enough? Well below the wrists even over the vest? Good. Are the sleeves gusseted at the wrists, and do the cuffs have *Velcro* closures so you can alter the tightness of the cuff at will? Good.

Now for a few subtleties. Are there any metal or plastic dingbats—snaps, cord locks, zipper sliders—that touch your hide when the parka's zipped up and the hood is drawn around your face? If there are, and the garment is otherwise acceptable, can this problem be corrected easily? Do the pockets have reliable, snow-proof closures? Some parkas have four bellows pockets on the front; some have three and one zippered breast pocket; some have two and one zippered breast pocket. The zippered pocket almost always has a vertical or slightly less than vertical zipper with a double flap arrangement to exclude snow. If it doesn't, it should. The bellows pockets should either have large flaps with generous *Velcro* tabs or **two** snaps on them to exclude snow, or should be of a sort that rolls down in sort of a seal (like rolling up a paper bag around a sandwich) and then is fastened. A pocket full of snow is a soggy horror, believe me!

Which brings up another point. Some parkas have the handwarmer pockets behind the lower bellows pockets, and/or slits that enable you to get to your pants pockets without hitching up the skirt of the parka. These are fine if they're either closed with a snap or a Velcro tab (I prefer Velcro), or provided with a generous flap. If it looks like snow can leak in around there, chances are that it will.

A useful modification that you can carry out at home is the addition of *Velcro* tabs to the outside back of your parka hood and to the inside of the parka's collar, or more specifically, to where the collar would be if it had a collar. This will enable you to roll the hood up inside itself, and fasten down so it won't fill up with snow blowing off of trees and such. It's one of those little luxuries that won't take you much time to make. Just be sure that the *Velcro* hooks are on the back of the parka hood and the *Velcro* "fur" is on the collar; otherwise you'll wind up with a neck-scratcher that's always on duty.

A Few Words About *Gore-Tex®*

Among the outdoor person's dreams has been the water-proof fabric that's also breathable. The combination of virtues isn't difficult to achieve in theory. All you need is a fabric with pores sufficiently large to transmit water vapor and sufficiently small to exclude water droplets. This isn't easy, because a water molecule has an effective diameter of about 2.76×10^{-8}cm. Nature helps, though, since water molecules like each other. The hydrogen atoms of one molecule are attracted by the hydrogen atoms of another molecule. This so-called "hydrogen bonding" keeps the molecules together. The strength of this bond determines the size that a drop of water will form on a macroscopic level. At any rate, the drop of water formed by the hydrogen bond is rather larger than the pore size of *Gore-Tex*®, the "heart" of which is a thin film of expanded polytetrafluorethylene. Teflon. Just like the stuff on your frying pan, but stretched out into tiny interlocking fibers and nodules. The film is very strong for all its seeming fragility. As the viscous strand of Teflon is stretched rapidly, tiny micropores open up in the structure. At the same time, the adjacent molecules align themselves in the direction of pull. The elongated fibers are, as a result, very strong.

A *Gore-Tex*® garment is actually a laminate of breathable ripstop nylon or high-count taffeta, a thin *Gore-Tex*® membrane, and depending on application, either a third layer of nylon or a non-directional polyester fabric. The purpose of the third layer is primarily to protect the PTFE membrane. Moisture transmission and water entry pressure isn't substantially different between the three-layer laminates and a two-layer laminate. But the difference in water entry pressure and vapor transmission between a *Gore-Tex*® laminate and other materials in common use for rain protection is impressive. The table tells the story. The higher the water entry pressure, the more "waterproof" the material; the higher the vapor transmission figure, the more "breathable" the material.

Material	Water Entry Pressure, PSI	Water Vapor Transmission GM/M²/24 hours
Nylon/Gore-Tex/ Non-directional polyester	60	4560
Nylon/Gore-Tex/Nylon	55	4806
Nylon/Gore-Tex	55	5080
Nylon, thermoplastic polyurethane coated	30	497
Nylon, thermoset polyurethane coated	60	74
Ventile (English)	2	4371
Venture Cloth (Howe & Bainbridge, USA)	2	4987
Gore-Tex® film	61	11,072

The data, taken from the results of tests performed by W. L. Gore & Associates, are impressive, but I can hear you saying under your breath, "Fine, but those tests were run by the dudes who made the stuff." Right. They were. So let's go back to the field. I've been wearing a Synergy Works Ventile Cloth parka for a few years now. It's a five-layer garment. The upper body, hood and arms are constructed of a layer of Ventile, a layer of circular weave netting used as a sleeping bag baffle material, a layer of Ventile, another layer of netting, and an inner liner of a marvelously soft nylon called *Kensuede-E*, a Howe and Bainbridge fabric developed originally for ski outerwear. As you can see from the tables, Ventile has a very low water entry pressure. However, the pressure increases as the fibers of the fabric grow damp and swell up. Furthermore, the mesh reduces layer contact and cuts down on the amount of water transmitted from one layer to another. The parka is dry, absolutely windproof and warm. It'a also hideously expensive and quite heavy.

Last summer, I began wearing a similarly cut Synergy Works parka in a laminate of nylon, *Gore-Tex*® and non-directional polyester, with an inner shell of *Kensuede-E* for additional warmth and comfort. The seams were sealed at the factory, so I didn't have to do that not-unpleasant task. *Gore-Tex*® laminates will leak around needle holes, and must be sealed. I've worn this parka in violent downpours, in wet snow, in brutally cold weather with wind-blown powder, on cool, damp, drizzly days—in short, every time a good test situation presented itself. It has performed impeccably. I have yet to get wet, and with the exception of one session of hard practice in a 60-degree drizzle in a marathon canoe, I've yet to get damp from perspiration. The parka has underarm zippers, which greatly aid in ventilation, and a superb hood that will turn a rain or a snow without being completely battened down. Molly has worn a Sierra West *Gore-Tex*® parka under similar circumstances and reported the same results—and the Sierra West parka doesn't have underarm zippers. (It has, for the record, an excellent hood.)

I've also used two different *Gore-Tex*® tents, an Early Winters Light Dimension two-person job and a big four person dome, the Makalu IV, from Lowe Alpine Systems. I managed to avoid bad weather with the Early Winters tent, but the big Lowe has caught all sorts of hell and remained dry and comfortable.

In short, the material **works.** So what, you say? Who needs rain protection in winter? You do, my friend. So do I. It can rain in winter, at surprisingly low temperatures. And wet snow is the physical equivalent of rain as far as your clothing goes. When I can wear a parka that's as windproof as any other parka, that transmits water vapor as well as any other parka, and that turns water aside as well as any other parka, I'm going to wear it! And as soon as I can afford overpants made of a *Gore-Tex®* laminate, I'm going to carry a pair with me on every winter trip. The stuff works. That's all this old man needs to know!

Insulated Garments

The casual winter daytripper can, as we've already discussed, function nicely with insulation layers found in the closet. A stout wool shirt, with a sweater in a daypack, and a good mountain parka as a first line of defense, can do the job in all but the bitterest weather.

However, the pattern of the wilderness recreationist is to go out further and in deeper as he or she gains confidence. Winter hiking is no exception. I suspect that we all share a desire to see what's over the next hill, or what's around the bend in the trail. And sooner or later, you'll be tempted by a winter overnight. At that point, you'll find that the insulation layers made up of shirts and sweaters are certainly amply warm, but bulky to carry in an already crowded pack, and heavy in terms of their thickness.

The answer is an insulation layer of down or polyester. Chances are that if you've done much three-season backpacking, you already have one of the two basic garments—a vest, or a jacket that's essentially a vest with sleeves.

You're not looking for an expedition-grade parka at this point in time. You may find that you're sufficiently engrossed in winter hiking to want to extend your range to wherever there's snow. But at this point, you're better advised to spend your bucks on a more flexible insulation system consisting of a lighter jacket or vest and a good mountain parka. By the time you're ready for a superjacket, you'll know what your needs are without being told.

I've used both down and polyester outerwear successfully, and as I own both (remember, this is my business as well as my avocation), I've evolved a simple rule. If it looks to be a dry, cool day—or a dry, cold couple of days—I'll carry down.

If it's over +20°F or damp or snowing or there's a frontal system on the way, I carry polyester. I'm a Northeasterner, which means that there's always a frontal system scratching at the door and meowing to be let in; in short, I carry polyester insulation most of the time. Polyester is bulkier, but not by much, and that difference is more than offset by the facts that it doesn't collapse when wet, and it retains full loft (thickness) when very damp. If this be heresy, then so be it. You can get orthodox opinions anywhere.

Shopping for a suitable jacket or parka is primarily shopping for a suitable fit, all other factors being rather equal. Chances are that you won't be wearing this secondary insulation layer on the trail, for reasons we've already discussed. This means that you can afford a somewhat more conforming fit—but not much more. You don't want an insulating layer so snug that the insulation gets compressed across your shoulders. Remember also that it must fit over a heavy undershirt, a wool shirt and maybe a sweater. So be sure to size it over those garments. Don't be embarrassed to do this in a mountain shop. It happens all the time, and the folks there are pleased that they don't have to guess on sizes for you.

What I look for in a vest is sufficient length, especially in the back. I prefer a vest that comes down well over the small of my back. I also like a stand-up collar that fits fairly snugly, which poses a problem. I'm as stringy as an eel, but have a thick neck for my size that's probably the result of a lot of hours in racing canoes; most collars are too tight for me unless I'm lucky—or unless I make the garment from a kit. I'm a terrible seamster (if "seamstress" exists, why not "seamster"?), but kit instructions have obviously been tested on a panel of TV game show watchers, and even I can follow them. My stitch lines wander a lot, but that doesn't hurt the warm of it none, good buddy.

So—long in the back, high and snug in the collar to keep in the warmth, and, as a final fillip, roomy enough in the armholes (scyes, in Garmentese) to permit movement without being so roomy that there's no insulation along your sides. I prefer snaps or *Velcro* tabs to a zipper, but when push comes to shove, I could care less. I'm also indifferent to pocket arrangement except around the house, where my matches and tobacco live in my vest. In our house, you wear a vest or heavy shirt in winter or you go broke heating the old white elephant.

A jacket may be more elaborate than a vest. Both are eminently practical garments that'll be worn for far more than just hiking. As the jacket may be your casual outerwear for a good chunk of winter, I'd suggest that it have a zipper and snap closure system, and that the pockets be covered with at least a flap to exclude blowing snow. Other than that, look for a snug collar and a comfortable fit with generously long sleeves. The longer jackets that cover your backside should be furnished with a waist drawcord and a double-bug zipper. The shorter jackets usually have a drawcord at the bottom, and it's useful when you're not moving around too much.

Most jackets come with insulated hoods available that snap onto the jacket, and for the few ounces they take to tote, they're worth the money. For the record, most snap-on hoods are lousy hoods. The drawcord is on the outer edge of the hood, and the hood is generally so skimpy that it wouldn't "tunnel" even if the drawcord were placed properly. But it's dependable warmth for the vital area of scalp and nape, and if the snow's blowing, your mountain parka hood, which does (or should) have a generous tunnel, will protect your face.

Most down vests and jackets are of sewn-through construction, which you're probably familiar with. If you're not, here's what's happening. Down, like geese, likes to migrate, and needs to be confined in small compartments. The simplest compartment is that formed when you stitch two pieces of fabric together in long tubes and fill the tubes. In cross-section, it looks like this:

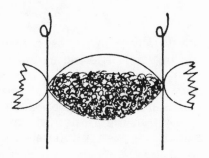

Obviously, no matter how much down you stuff into these tubes, your insulation dwindles to two thicknesses of nylon and a hank of thread between them. It's also evident that the insulation will fall away from the top of the tube a bit in use, like this:

The alternative, of course, is to build a jacket with compartments that look like boxes rather than envelopes, like this:

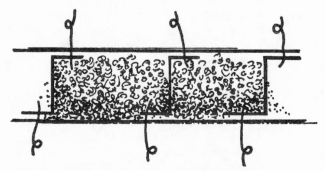

The baffles are usually of nylon mesh or nylon bobbinet or circular-weave polyester. The big expedition parkas are built like this, and it's desirable in terms of ultimate theoretical warmth. It's also a whole lot more expensive. Much of the heat loss at the seams in the sewn-through garment is overcome by that big, bulletproof mountain parka anyway, so while the box-construction parka is a beauty, you probably don't need it.

Take a few minutes to evaluate the construction of the jacket. Put it down on the counter and pat it to make sure the down is uniformly distributed, then hold it up to the light to see if the tubes are generaously filled. If they're only half-filled when the down is dry and well-distributed, it doesn't take much imagination to figure out what they'll look like when the down is damp and the jacket has lived in a small stuff bag for 12 hours!

Make sure that the zipper works freely, and that the snaps are well secured (and *snap,* too!). Check out the drawcords on the hood and the bottom (or middle) to see if they work. Sometimes one gets caught by a vagrant stitch, and the time to know that is before you put your money down.

Assessing the quality of the fill in the jacket is beyond what you and I can do in the store. Price is generally a good indication of fill quality. I hate to say it, but it's true. If two jackets of comparable shell quality and needlework are selling at grossly disparate prices, there has to be a reason. The store might have managed to cop some jackets in the off-season at a favorable price, in which case you may have a genuine good buy in your hands. Or it may be that one jacket is made with shoddy shell material and mediocre down. You **can** count threads, if you wish, and you can assume that a jacket made of sleazy nylon is filled with sleazy down.

On the other hand, you know that Camp 7, Class 5, Gerry, North Face, Sierra Designs and Snow Lion, who are major suppliers of garments to outdoor shops, are building a down garment that represents good value for your dollars. Sure, they're building gear to make a profit, but profit in itself isn't an ugly word. If nobody made a profit in the needle trades, we'd all still be wearing homespun! What I'm saying is that you can trust most manufacturers to supply quality commensurate with cost of manufacture. There are few shortcuts or "trade secrets" in the garment industry, and the production boss at, say, Camp 7, can tell you to the minute the needle time in, say, a North Face jacket or vest if he or she disassembles it. It's a competitive business, and the folks who overprice their goods in terms of perceived value don't stay around long.

One puzzler to a lot of folks is the small manufacturer that they've never heard of. If you read *Wilderness Camping* or *Backpacker,* you'll find a lot of ads from a lot of small shops who build gear for a limited market or for sale direct to the consumer. It's typically expensive gear, and typically superb gear as well. The best down jackets and sleeping bags I've seen in the past five years have come from a tiny outfit called Marmot Mountain Works in Grand Junction, Colorado. Their specialty is high quality down encased in *Gore-Tex®* shells.

Their prices are astronomical, and their quality has to be seen to be believed. They're not alone, either. There's a lot of righteous gear out there. All you need is money.

Which brings up another point. Good gear can be costly. Bad gear, obviously, is more expensive, because you've wasted the money you spent on something that doesn't do the job, and you **still** have to buy something that does the job. Over the long haul, well-sewn, well-designed gear isn't that all-fired costly. If a well-made mountain parka costs $70 and a shoddy one $40, but the useful life of the good one is ten years and the shoddy one four years (assuming it has any truly useful life), the good coat is costing you seven bucks a year as opposed to ten for the mediocre one. And in four years, a mediocre replacement for the mediocre original may have gone up in price to $70 anyway! The moral of this story is that you should consider carefully what you need, buy only what you need, buy no bells and whistles that won't be useful, and buy the best you can afford that suits your needs. You'll save money in the long run, and your gear will do the job better every time it's called on.

If there is controversy about down garments, the controversy about polyester garments could only be called a full-out firefight. Not only are there two giants competing for the basic insulation trade, but there are some radically different ways of handling these materials on the cutting table. Like everybody else, I have a few opinions of my own, which we'll talk over in a while.

If you remember, Du Pont's *Hollofil II* is a chopped staple fiber. Each strand is short. Celanese's *Polarguard* is a continuous filament fiberfill that is supplied in rolls like a blanket, as it were. Both are essentially equivalent in insulation value. Both are durable. *Hollofil II*, being chopped staple, requires restraint in application. It must be quilted for jackets and vests, otherwise it will sag and migrate much like down, although not nearly as dramatically. *Polarguard*, on the other hand, lends itself to edge stabilization, in which the bat of continuous filaments is sewn to the shell only at the seams. It can, of course, be quilted—and usually is. It can also be laminated. These options can present the buyer with some interesting choices, to say the least. Finally, *Polarguard*, being a continuous filament bat rather than a chopped fiber, can provide a somewhat more uniform insulation thickness with less manufacturing fuss (for which read $$). But the tradeoffs don't end here. My experience has been that *Hollofil II* has a little more flexibility and a more pleasant "hand" than *Polarguard,* and I suspect that it's a bit more compressible in the field if not in terms of laboratory data.

Compairsons are interesting, but the basic point is that polyester insulation **works.** It retains its loft when wet. Polyester dries readily because it absorbs essentially no moisture. It's far less expensive than down. It doesn't rot, mold or mildew because the beasties that create those events can't eat the stuff. Polyester appears to be long-lived in the field, and it certainly has proven to be long-lived in accelerated lab tests. It's not the optimum insulation in terms of volume per unit weight, but it's good.

The criteria for choosing a polyester-insulated garment are the same as those you'd use for selecting a down garment. In brief, it has to fit properly and if it has bells and whistles on it, the bells have to ding and the whistles have to toot. Beyond that, you're mostly in the realm of theoretical considerations and dollar tradeoffs, particularly with *Polarguard.*

Hollofil II's easy to analyze. Is it thick enough? Is it uniform? Are the tubes well filled? Fine. No problem. *Polarguard's* a bucket of worms in comparison. Fortunately, most garments that you'll be looking at are simplly quilted before manufacture (in bolts) and the quilted material (shells and insulation) are cut and sewn. You know that the thickness is uniform except at the quilt line, and you know that even then it's not absolutely zero, like a sewn-through seam in a down garment. You also know that cutting a garment results in a lot of scrap. Scrap when you're cutting a pre-quilted bat is very expensive scrap. It's less expensive than if you were doing the same quilting in-house, garment by garment, because you're swapping uncomplicated needlework for fancy needlework, which still is costly.

The other factor to consider is in part theoretical, but still operative on a practical level. *Polarguard* will grow thicker after several washings. The reason is that a resin is sprayed on the blanket as the material is blown from the tow. This resin keeps the fibers together to facilitate handling and cutting, and it will wash out quickly. As it washes out, the fibers expand as though they were unglued. The result is a thicker insulation layer—which is to say a warmer insulation layer. Quilting inhibits this growth in thickness to some degree, and some people in the trade also claim that restraining the fibers by relatively closely-spaced quilt lines inhibits the material's loft and compressibility, and may be detrimental to its longevity as well.

These folks opt for lamination, a costly process, but one which permits the full growth of the fibers after washing, and also minimizes any chance of the bat separating or developing thin spots after long, hard use.

The material is actually laminated at two points. The first lamination is of the outer shell material to the insulation. This is **not** a permanent bond, and is **not intended to be** a permanent bond. It's done to facilitate subsequent handling of the material. If you're curious, it isn't a permanent bond because it would serve no useful purpose. The **useful** lamination (except in terms of cutting costs, which is useful to you too, of course) is a thin layer of non-woven polyester to which the insulation blanket is **permanently** bonded with a very flexible adhesive. This means that the insulation will resist separation and pulling apart even more than it does in an unlaminated state, and that its expansion after washing is controlled directionally. It can only grow fatter.

Lamination is expensive, more so than quilting, and the cutting scrap is no less, surely. Production time—the actual time spent cutting and assembling the garment, is less with a laminated bat than with a quilted bat, but not enough to offset the greater cost of lamination. This means that you'll either pay more for a laminated *Polarguard* garment, or you'll get less exotic fittings. There isn't any free lunch. This may all be changed shortly, though, by the development of a new laminating plant that will make use of up-to-date technology, and hopefully reduce costs of lamination a fair bit.

The other option is edge stabilization, in which a shell and insulation laminate (**not** permanent—intended to facilitate cutting only) is cut into patterned pieces which are sewn at the seams only. This results in a low-cost garment, but one that's subject to separation of the insulation layers—or so I've been told. It's never happened to me, and the whole family has been beating up on one edge-stabilized *Polarguard* mummy bag for three years. The kids use it all winter in the house! However, *Polarguard* isn't indestructible, and I suppose that the edge-stabilized bat could be separated to produce a thin spot. □

TENTS AND OTHER SHELTERS

The winter backpacker needs shelter. It's equally obvious that tents designed for winter or expedition use are very, very expensive. You **pay** for those snow flaps and tunnel entrances and frost liners and cookholes—in money and in weight. If you plan to do a lot of winter backpacking, or if you find that you like winter camping and plan to take it up "seriously," the investment in an honest-to-God winter tent is worthwhile if your summer tent is marginal. Most folks, happily, will find that their summer tent is useful if: 1) it's a breathable tent with a separate waterproof fly, 2) the pole system and pitching method is adaptable to snow camping, and 3) if it's big enough.

The last is the easiest to cope with. There's no law that requires a winter tent to be big enough to contain the packs of the folks using it, but once you've grown accustomed to that luxury, it's one that's terribly hard to give up. The reasons are obvious. You won't wake up in the morning to find your pack buried under eighteen inches of cold, wet snow—and when you dig it out, it's inevitable that you left the pocket containing your dry socks and dry mittens open. AARRGH! What's that about the best laid plans of mice and men? The other equally obvious reason is that it's most pleasant to have your portable wardrobe and snack bar at your side. Meandering out to dig up your fresh undershirt on a chilly morning isn't my idea of fun and games.

Now back to Number One. If you choose to use a tent for winter camping—and I choose to, believe me!—you need a double-walled tent, unless your three-season tent is made of *Gore-Tex*. You've heard this song before, but I'll tell you again because it's important.

A tent, by virtue of the facts that it's windproof and occupied by warm bodies, is warmer inside than the ambient air. That warm air also carries a fair amount of moisture around in the form of your breath and your perspiration. This moisture will condense on the cold wall of the tent to a greater or lesser extent. If the tent body is impermeable, the condensation will build up to an impressive layer of frost, which will either melt and drip on you or will be deposited on you in the form of a mini-snowstorm and melt on your gear if it's warm enough.

Don't be misled by the idea that an uncoated tent body or a *Gore-Tex* tent body will not develop a condensation build-up. They will—and I've had people come a'roarin' and a'stompin' into my shop in the old days telling me that their new tent didn't work; that there was a frost buildup on the tent body. And I have to go through the whole damn routine again, including giving the dude *another* one-page handout I'd prepared to tell him that his tent wasn't perfectly breathable when he'd bought the thing. Some condensation will occur in the best of tents. It's just that a lot more occurs in single-wall coated nylon tents. But—as long as there's fabric between you and the outdoors, and a temperature diffeential, some condensation will take place.

Of course, you can live with heavy condensation. It's not pleasant, and it means turning the tent inside-out to shake the stuff loose—a good idea at any time with any tent—but you can live with it. The problem is that the tents most prone to heavy condensation, the inexpensive (relatively!) coated nylon jobs, generally aren't designed to be pitched in snow. They're designed around a single pole fore and aft that lifts the ridge, and this pole tends to sink out of sight in snow. Of course you can tether the peaks to some friendly local trees—but 1) there's never a tree where you want it, and 2) even after you've strung it to a tree, the structure is shaky enough that it will wobble, schwobble, list to port and suffer keenly if a heavy snow comes down. You need something that's more stable as well as something that's more breathable. Chances are that you already have a good, solid basic A-frame or A-frame front and single stub pole rear tent that you use for three-season backpacking. If you don't, now's the time to consider one—or to consider one of the many domes, wedges and modified domes on the market.

The dome and its cousins have a marvelous advantage for the winter camper. They're essentially freestanding. Granted, you'll find a need to tether one down if you're in a camp that's exposed to the wind, but if you're just getting into winter backpacking, you won't be making camp in lofty, exposed places anyway. By the time you're ready for that kind of stuff, you'll have discovered thirty-eleven ways to secure a tent in snow. I'll tell you a few of them; after all, you should be free to experience the joy of discovery yourself. Don't worry, though—what I won't tell you won't diminish either your safety or your pleasure.

If there's a "secret" to pitching a tent on snow, it's this— start with a firm platform. Truck around on your skis or your snowshoes, pack out the kitchen and the tent area and pack out a trail to the area you'll use as a latrine. Be meticulous; be thorough—which means, get to camp on time! Pack the kitchen first, so the cook can start to work, and then do the rest. The tent should be up and the bags out and fluffed at about just enough time before chow call to change into a dry undershirt and a heavy parka.

Why all this packing and repacking? First, a solid foundation is most pleasant to walk on around camp. Remember, you won't be wearing your skis or snowshoes, and if you don't pack things down thoroughly, you'll sink up to your thighs with each step. Winter hikers call it "postholing"—and it's a helluva way to run a railroad, believe me! Second, as you sleep, you'll compress the snow beneath you. If you start with semi-fluff, you'll find that the heavier parts of your body settle very deeply indeed into the snow and the rest of you "floats." If you don't pack down the snow under your tent, you'll end up like a jackknife.

If the snow is well packed, it's possible to secure a tent floor and sidepulls with the small skewers that come with the tent. The route to take here is to stop the snow even more firmly and set the skewer all the way in. The compacted snow will solidify even more in a few minutes, and the pegs will be held securely. A conventional A-frame may require a more rigid attachment for the forepeak pullouts. Two trees are useful, but not always available unless you've packed a couple of lengths (20 footers are fine) of chute cord that you can attach to the forepeak pullouts and lengthen them. Skis make admirable trees if the snow is deep, as do ski poles, snowshoes and ice axes. If the snow isn't deep enough, you may be able to bury your ski poles or skis. Arrange them in the form of an X, and attach the pullout rope to the junction.

Another useful tool is the *Frisbee*. Please don't use a Master or a Professional or a Moonlighter; get a pair of cheap ones. Cut a slit from the corner to the middle or drill a hole in the middle of the *Frisbee*, slip the cord in or through, secure the rope on the far side of the *Frisbee* by half-hitching a stick, bury the setup at a 45° angle and stomp the snow down well. It works. So does a snowshoe if you either bury it and fasten the rope to the crosspiece, or stick its nose deep into the snow at an angle with the rope attached to the nose.

By the way, I prefer drilling a *Frisbee* to slitting it. A drill hole can be covered with tape and you can play *Frisbee* on snowshoes, which rivals *Frisbee* in canoes as a singularly joyous, whacky pastime.

So much for the tent. While I could rattle about a lot of theoretical schlog, I don't think it's of any consequence in the real world. A breathable tent—and yes, do bring the rainfly and please use it—a firmly packed tent platform and a modicum of good sense in pitching it will result in a snug, happy camp.

I should say something about selecting a campsite in winter. Perhaps I was too rash in assuming that you'd figure that out, because the rules aren't the same as they are in summer. There's no point in selecting an open, breezy site to reduce the insect population. On the other hand, be very wary of groves of big hardwoods. You can't always spot the dead ones easily, and just as many limbs fall in winter as in summer.

Even a small object can raise a fair welt. A few hours ago, I was walking a trail back from a high bluff overlooking Tennessee's Obed River, a monumentally beautiful whitewater stream and the state's first Federal wild river, with Bob Lantz and Roy, Juanita and Margie Guinn from the Tennessee Scenic Rivers Association, which spearheaded the thrust to preserve this spectacular area. Simply stated, I was bonked on the head by an acorn that fell from a big oak, and I can still feel the lump as I sit writing this chapter on my flight back from Knoxville. Watch out for big dead trees.

Shelter from the wind is eminently desirable. I like to hunt out a little snuggle of conifers, myself, provided I can prepare a kitchen of something approaching suitable size. It isn't always easy, as I like a big tent in winter even for just Molly and me. (Yeah, we break the Rule of Four at times, but only in easy country that's accessible to our car and to assistance if one of us should require it. But then, I'm writing the book as a winter camper, not reading it as a beginner.) With a party, it's even less easy—which is one of the compelling arguments for making camp early. If we're skiing, we'll often set up camp at our lunch break and spend the afternoon skiing short out-and-backs from the camp, carrying our emergency gear in fanny packs. It's a lot more pleasant than having to make camp when you're tired, and it's a lot more fun to ski without a pack. When we're snowshoeing, we'll usually try to set up camp by about 4:00 if not earlier. It should be obvious by now that ol' HNR isn't a fan of long, grim marches to arrive at a predetermined destination unless it's absolutely necessary for the safety of the party.

One thing that'll make me camp somewhere other than in my favorite cluster of small conifers is the presence of running water. If you know your terrain, you'll be able to spot streams even if they're covered with snow and a shell of ice. Streamwalking in winter is always hazardous, but some judicious poking with a ski pole or an ice axe may uncover the winter camper's greatest labor-saver, running water. I still won't break the dead tree rule to be next to running water, and there ain't no way you'll ever find me camped on or at the base of any steep slope that can hold a lot of snow. Mountaineers may have to expose themselves to avalanche hazards as an inevitable concomitant of finding any shelter—I don't have to. Recognizing a potentially hazardous slope requires a fair degree of experience—but it doesn't take any experience if you remember that any steep, open slope covered with snow can slide—and a few trees are no guarantee either. A big climax avalanche can toss around mature Ponderosa pines like jackstraws. Even a tiny slough avalanche can toss you around.

There are other shelters beside tents, as you can well imagine. The hardy opt for a tarp and a bivouac sack (a coated nylon or *Gore-Tex* overbag) for their sleeping bag. It's not an unpleasant way to sleep on a still night, and the display of stars overhead is unlike anything you'll ever see. All you have to do is peek around the corner of your roof! The inveterate winter bum will make a snow house, and while I can tell you how to make a snow house, I'd rather advise you to get a skinny little book called *Igloos* from *Off Belay*, 15630 S.E. 124th St., Renton, WA 98055, a very fine climbing and mountaineering magazine that specializes in the Pacific Northwest. Ray Smutek is the editor, and Ray knows his trade so well that no nonsense gets into the pages. The book will cost you the princely sum of seventy five cents, and if you're into the same head that I am about winter, you'll be out there on your front lawn building a snow house just for practice, at least once this winter. In fact, it's a good idea to practice this skill before you go bopping off into the boonies to use it. Make your mistakes where it doesn't matter first—and besides, the kids will have a ball helping you! Mine do, at any rate.

The one shelter beside a tent that you really should know how to manage is the snow cave. Why? It's simple, adaptable to the terrain, quickly prepared with minimal gear, and it may bail you and your companions out of a tough situation some day.

The simplest form of snow cave isn't a cave at all. It's a trench scooped out of the snow and covered with some branches and boughs over which you throw some snow. Crawl in, arrange your sleeping gear, toss a groundcloth (or even an empty pack) up against the entry (make sure you have an airway that a snowfall won't plug up!) and presto, there's your very own sleeping room, insulated by snow and protected from the wind. If the snow is deep, you can pack the area before you excavate the trench and even dig a ramp or steps out. If you have a convenient sidehill or a big old Adirondack boulder, you can heap up snow against it, pack it, and dig out a cave in the pile. This is more elaborate, and at best is a wet, messy, fatiguing operation that's less well suited to the needs of a tired, hungry party that's forced to bivouac.

There are exceptions to this rule, of course.

If one member of the party is injured, the relative security of the cave may make its construction imperative. If it looks like you're going to be socked in for a day or two by a heavy storm, it may be well worth the energy expenditure to have the whole party together and secure, providing physical and psychological warmth for each other. But for the quick shelter for a tired party, or a party caught out too far and forced to bivouac, the trench is the quickest and simplest and least wasteful of dwindling energy.

Trenches and caves can certainly be prepared admirably with snowshoes. As more and more people are using touring skis, some forethought should be taken regarding emergency shelter construction. A ski is a *lousy* shovel! In rugged terrain, I'd consider carrying a small pair of webs for each party of ski tourers just to simplify making camp and for possible emergency use, regardless of how adept the individuals may be on skis. For an extended trip, a couple of pairs of webs for a party of four might not be amiss. Don't get me wrong. The ski is a marvelous instrument of travel—and I much prefer skis to snowshoes in most terrain—but in camp, the webs are better. And a snowshoe is a better shovel than a ski tip, a small pot, or mittened hands!

Of course, a shovel is best yet, and lots of mountain shops carry little French-made aluminum shovels with demountable handles that have been used by generations of Alpinists. The one catalogued by Eastern Mountain Sports has a blade that's 7½ inches wide and 9½ inches deep, and weighs, with a 14 inch handle, a tidy 21 ounces. If you're carrying an ice axe, you'll probably find that the little shovel will fit nicely over the spike end of the axe, and you can leave the handle at home. EMS also sells a big aluminum snow anchor that can be fitted with a handle. They also sell a snow saw for cutting blocks to make snow houses, if you're into that type of fun. The point of all this is that the shovel is a useful tool that more than makes up for its weight in energy saved if you need to construct a trench shelter.

While we're on the subject of shelters, I'd like to put in a good word for the bivouac bag. This is a sack that fits over your sleeping bag and is made either of coated nylon on the bottom and uncoated on the top or of *Gore-Tex*. Its adaptability as emergency shelter is obvious; its use as primary shelter is obvious. Less obvious is the fact that it adds a few degrees of protection to your sleeping bag even in the snug confines of a tent, and it keeps your bag a little drier and less subject to the whims and vagaries of blown snow and spilled Sherpa tea. I think of a bivvy sack as part of my primary shelter arrangement as well as my emergency shelter. If you start using one, you'll be most reluctant to do without it, believe me.

Oh, yes—one more piece of advice. I'm not a lover of open flame in a tent, although I'm aware that a lot of very experienced folks do cook in a tent on a winter trip.

I'm less disturbed by open flame in a snow house or snow cave, provided that 1) the shelter is well ventilated and 2) it's cold enough outside to freeze the walls after the flame is extinguished. In fact, this is a time-honored way to turn a snow house into a nearly bombproof ice house, which makes a desirable base camp for long stays in the boonies.

However, there's one form of flame that I like in a tent or a small snow cave, and that's the small, cylindrical French candle lantern. The flame is well shielded, and virtually idiotproof. It makes a cheery glow in the early evening, enough to read by, in fact, and it will raise the temperature of a tent interior or a snow cave appreciably. One little candle in an aluminum and glass house can buy you ten degrees in a tent and up to thirty degrees in a snow cave! A worthwhile five ounces they are, believe me! And a spot of cheer when the dark chill of night settles in. □

SLEEPING BAGS AND SUCH

Back when I was an outfitter and had to work for a living, it always bothered me to have to tell customers who wanted to go winter camping that their most important purchase wasn't a big, fat, expensive sleeping bag. Don't misunderstand me. I have no objection at all to being swathed in goosedown 10 inches thick—and I had no objection then to taking the huge sum of money that such a bag represented. But a winter bag isn't a first purchase. Bags rank well down the list, behind boots, underwear, mittens, hat, shell parka, winter stove and a lot of other things. This is, in brief, a luxury for the occasional winter backpacker and a necessity only for those who must part with the dollars to optimize their gear for difficult long-term trips in high and remote places.

There is obviously justification for the honest-to-God winter bag if you're an expedition mountaineer or if you have the dollars to make your load a little lighter. Let's assume, however, that you're an ordinary citizen who backpacks in three seasons in the Northeast, Midwest or Appalachian highlands. Chances are pretty good that you own a sleeping bag that's comfortable to at least 25°F, and probably lower than that. Chances are also good that it's a mummy bag. Whether it's down, synthetic, or steel wool is of no consequence. All that matters is that you're warm in it when the frost is on the pumpkin—because we're going to use that as the basis for a winter sleeping bag that'll work in the Adirondacks, the White Mountains, and even in Bemidji, Minnesota, where gasoline's a buck-two-eighty and you can get busted for smuggling lignonberries.

Drag out your good ol' three season sleeper and either trundle it down to your friendly local outfitter's or break open a mail order catalog. We're going to find another sleeping bag that yours will either fit inside of or that you can stuff into yours, depending on the size of your bag, or your size, and your preferences regarding comfort. I'd look for a synthetic bag, with or without a hood, that by itself would keep me warm at around 40° with a pad under me. I could be talked into a down bag if weight was a really important factor, but I'd opt for the synthetic, based on both cost and "warmth when damp" considerations.

I'll use a couple of our bags as examples. Molly uses a Camp 7 North Col, which is a very skinny down mummy that's warm to about 10° above for her. It's narrow enough that she can fit it inside of a summer-weight *Polarguard* mummy of mine. The combination of the two has proven to be warm **(for her!)** to -20°F, and would probably be warmer than that if she chose to camp out at such insanely low temperatures. I have a roomy *Polarguard* mummy that I can fit a slim summer-weight synthetic mummy inside of, and this combination, which could be bought today for under $110, keeps me warm at that same -20°F. I could, of course, take a legitimate three-season bag like my old Sierra #100 and put a very slim Camp 7 synthetic mummy inside it—a bag that was designed as a liner for other sleepers, including a synthetic outer that Camp 7 builds—throw the whole shebang into a bivouac cover, and I'd be set for just about any temperature that I might encounter anywhere in the Northern Hemisphere. Sure, this array weighs more than, say, a Sierra Designs Nimbus—but the Nimbus is selling for a mere $300 in regular size. Granted that's a pretty spectacular sack—but a substantial mummy bag usable in most winter conditions will set you back around $200. I'd rather modify what I already have, thank you, unless I was deeply committed to winter trips. Even then, the combination inner and outer bag, with one of them a synthetic bag, offers the advantages of flexibility and that margin of safety that only the synthetics afford.

But the sleeping bag itself is only a part of a total sleeping system for the winter backpacker. The other parts of the system are a bivouac sack, a closed-cell foam pad, a hat, and some extra clothing if required. The foundation is the closed-cell foam pad. This is the major barrier between you and all of that cold, cold ground. The finest down in the world will compress under you to virtually nothing; the synthetics, while better, still compress a good bit. Thickness is warmth. The only way you're going to achieve that warmth is to use that relatively incompressible barrier of closed-cell foam under you.

Why closed-cell foam? Well, the air matress is thick enough, but the air circulates inside it, and ultimately will transfer heat from a small, warm you to a large, cold earth. Open-celled foam—the comfortable polyethylene pad covered with waterproof nylon—isn't really happy at low temperatures. It compresses—which is what makes it comfortable—and it permits some air circulation. It also absorbs moisture—and moisture increases the transfer rate of heat away from your body. The mountaineer's rule of thumb is that 2 inches of open-celled foam is the insulation equivalent of a half inch of closed-cell foam.

I've used half inch thick *Ensolite* for many years for winter trips, and it's served me well. This winter, I plan to use a relatively new foam, also closed-cell, called *Volarafoam,* which is lighter than *Ensolite,* reputedly less resistant to abrasion, and certainly cheaper. Abrasion resistance is a trivial concern in winter camping. And, frankly, it's equally trivial in 3-season camping. You're not going to chew up a foam pad in two weeks!

All this is by way of saying that we're making a person sandwich. The outer layer is a bivouac sack. The next layer, between the sleeping bag(s) and the bivvy sack, is the closed-cell foam pad. Next comes the sleeping bag array—and next comes you—with or without clothes.

It is not an act of heresy to wear clothing in a sleeping bag. In summer it's superfluous, generally, but in winter, a dry set of long johns is a distinct comfort, especially when you have to get up. The key is to crawl into the sack wearing **dry** (or mostly dry!) underclothing. Experts say that wearing even slightly damp long johns is a no-no. I just go ahead and do it anyway, and I haven't been aware of any dramatic deterioration of my insulation.

If it's bitter out, and your sleeping gear is marginal, long johns are most useful. So are socks—dry ones. So, too, is a hat. As I've said before, this furry-faced outdoor magazine editor wears a nightcap. Wears, not drinks. But that's another discussion.

What if it's **really** bitter, though. Can you use those clothes you have in your pack? Sure you can use them. It's evident that a sweater or a shirt can be most useful as additional insulation. An insulated jacket is too easily compressed if you wear it—but laid out between the sleeping bag and the bivvy cover, or laid out between you and the top of the sleeping bag, it buys you a good chunk of warmth.

A few other hints are in order here. The typical foam pad is a 60-inch long device, which may cover most of you, but doesn't cover me. Specifically, it leaves my feet a-dangle on the cold, cold ground. A mountain parka under your bivvy bag, though, will afford excellent insulation, as will a big subframed rucksack. In fact, you can even put your sleeping bag into the top of some big rucksacks! Granted, the big rucksack doesn't offer a huge amount of insulation, but it's better than the cold, cold ground. I spruce up the thermal values a bit, though, by putting a small chunk of closed-cell foam inside the rucksack. This is my Sit-Upon, and it occupies an honored spot on the top of my rucksack where it's accessible whenever I park my skinny butt on a cold log for a rest and a mug-up. Used in the rucksack, I suppose I should call it a Foot-Upon. It also gets used under my food to preserve some tiny semblances of warmth at times, in which case it should be called a Pot-Upon. And if I carry this much further, you'll begin to feel Put-Upon.

Sorry. That's what happens when you become addicted to writing late at night.

All this improvisation with an existing sleeping bag and a low-priced inner or outer bag is fine—but I suspect that some of you may be thinking that your summer bag is pretty old or marginal for three season hiking, and that you'd like the excuse to treat yourself to a new bag for winter. What to do then, pray tell? Well, pretty much the same thing, except new. I'd start off with a reasonably generously-cut three-season mummy bag in down or synthetic (or the Jan Sport hybrid bag, with down on top and synthetic underneath—a luxurious sack), and I'd find a skinny synthetic mummy to fit inside it. Why synthetic inside? That's where most of the moisture's going to go. The synthetic fill won't collapse if it gets a little damp—neither will it reatin moisture for as long. Yet I'll confess that a down bag feels better as an inner bag. It conforms better, fills in the hollows better, and it's softer.

This way you have a luxurious three-season bag that's useful for a lot of winter camping and a summer bag that'll take a lot of beating—including immersion—for about the price of a good winter bag that's unbearable much above 40°. Of course, you're trucking around some more weight. The *pukka* winter bag will probably weight about 5½ pounds in down; the three-season bag will weigh around 4 pounds, as will the synthetic mummy. More weight and more bulk. If you can cope with that, it's a more versatile system. □

WITH MAP, COMPASS AND UNCOMMON SENSE

I've assumed all along in this book that you're a fairly well-seasoned backpacker. However, nothing's as expensive—or dangerous—as a fine, fat, full-blown assumption. Experienced outdoorspeople know how to use a map and a compass, right? Wrong! Some do. Most don't. If all your trekking has been on well-marked trails, you might never have had the necessity to work with a map and compass as if your life depended on it. Sure, you've probably been turned around in the outback just as I have, but in summer, in familiar terrain, it's hardly a major problem. There's hardly a valley in hiking country that doesn't have a trail running through it. With a little patience and some half-baked map and compass work, you can get squared away with hardly any hassle.

Winter's different. In our neck of the woods, trail markers may vanish in a deep snow, or enough of them may be obscured that you could stumble on a trail and follow it for several miles and not know it. You might not even recognize a fairly healthy small brook if there's six feet of snow on the ground! A lot of the familiar signposts (real and experiential) are obliterated in winter.

On the other hand, the hardwoods have shed their leaves. The blowdowns are snowed over. The waist-deep puckerbrush is a smooth expanse of snow. It's easier to see in winter, and easier to avail yourself of a route that would be a tangled horror in summer. All of which adds up to the fact that you'd better **know** how to use a map and a compass before you go out on a long trip—or even a short one in tough country.

If you have either Bjorn Kjellstrom's excellent *Be Expert With Map and Compass* or my very own *Movin' Out*, you can go back to them and refresh your skills. For the record, you'll learn more from Bjorn's book, but you'll learn enough more quickly from *Movin' Out*, Chapter 11. If you don't have either, give a listen.

The requisite skills for woods wandering aren't difficult to attain. Let's go down to your friendly local outfitter and buy two things, a map and a compass. The map's easy. Ask for the U.S. Geological Survey map for the area you live in, or for a nearby area if you're a city dweller. While you're getting the map, look at the index sheet that your outfitter probably has on display. There's your state, broken up in lots of little rectangles. They're not all the same size. If you're an Easterner, the boxes come in two sizes. The larger one is the so-called 15 minute sheet, because it covers fifteen minutes of longitude. The smaller ones, four of which are necessary to cover a 15 minute sheet, are 7½ minute sheets. USGS has embarked on a program to put the whole country on 7½ minute sheets, but you gotta be patient. The 7½ minute sheets have some definite advantages, as you can see. They're much easier to read. However, they cover such a small area that it's at times difficult to gain a broad view of the terrain. The 15-minute map is plotted on a scale of 1:62500, which means that one unit of measure on the map equals 62,500 units on the ground. This is close to the simple, easily remembered scale of one inch equals one mile. The 7½ minute sheet is plotted on a 1:24000 scale, or more simply, an inch equals 2,000 feet on the ground. Got your map? Fine. Now let's get a compass to go with the map.

You want a compass that's mounted on a transparent plastic plate to facilitate map work. You also want a liquid-filled compass, because the needle comes to rest much more quickly with this type than with the less expensive induction-damped unit, and it stays put so you can read it more accurately.

In the lower left hand margin of the map in front of you, there's technical information on how the mapping was done and to what bases. To the right of that is a little collection of lines and arcs that looks like a problem in geometry. It tells you that true north (straight up on the map) and magnetic north aren't the same in most places in North America, which means that your compass and your map aren't exactly in line unless you live along a wavy line that passes through such eminent wilderness areas as Grand Rapids, Michigan, and Knoxville, Tennessee. (East of Knoxville, up in the Cumberlands, is one of America's great undiscovered wildernesses, and marvelous winter hiking country it is. But that's another story.) The difference between your compass and your map is expressed in that angle called *declination*. You can adjust for this angle of declination with ease, without buying an expensive compass. The time will come when map and compass work sneaks up on you and you become a map

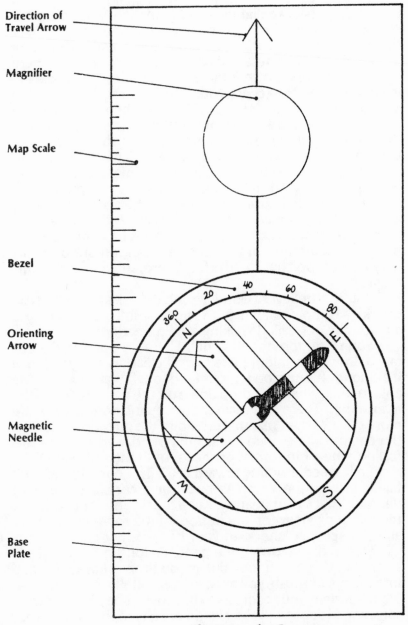

Direction of
Travel Arrow

Magnifier

Map Scale

Bezel

Orienting
Arrow

Magnetic
Needle

Base
Plate

The Parts of a Compass

freak, but that takes time. All you want for the present is that simple board-mounted, liquid-filled compass.

What your outfitter will probably hand you is a Silva Polaris, or possibly a slightly larger (and slightly more expensive) Silva model, although you may see a Suunto. You can't do any better for the price than any of these, and you can do a lot worse. Take a minute and check out your purchase. There isn't a bubble in the case, is there? Good. Does the needle swing freely? Fine. Now check your instrument against a handful of others in the dealer's supply. Don't set them side by side— they won't like that a bit. All of them point toward the bow of the Jensen competition cruising canoe on the wall? Good. Close enough. The compass works. Okay! No bubbles, no impairment in needle motion, general agreement as to the location of magentic north? You got yourself a compass.

The first step in using a compass is the acceptance of an article of faith. *The compass is always right.* There may be a time when it isn't. You could, for example, be standing over a heavy concentration of iron ore—although more probably it's your steel belt buckle. The first is rare, and the second correctable.

You're a believer? Good. Now let's look at what you can do with a compass and map. The first doesn't require a map at all, actually. It's called walking a field bearing.

You're on top of a little hill. There's a pond in the distance. In winter, it looks like a small clearing, but you know it's a pond. It's not too far, but far enough that you won't be able to see it when you drop down off the rise. It's not on the map, either. There's a stream shown, but no pond. Beaver are more diligent than mapmakers. Point the direction arrow on the compass base plate toward the pond, and turn the dial (called a bezel in formal parlance) until the red end of the magnetic needle points toward 360°. The direction arrow's tail intersects the compass bezel at a certain number of degrees. That's your bearing. Keep the magnetic needle over the orienting arrow on the bottom of the rotating bezel. It's an easy, accurate check on your heading.

Start walking toward the pond. As long as the pond's in sight, there's no problem, but as you drop off the ridge and into the puckerbush, you must rely on that skinny little arrow. Stop. Reorient your compass to the correct bearing just to be sure, and pick out a distinct landmark ahead that lies on your path of travel, like a big tree. Go to it, reorient again, pick another landmark, and keep on trucking. Sooner or later, you'll hit the pond.

There's also a simpler way. If that pond's a little five acre one two miles away, you could conceivably miss it if you tried to hit it accurately in the middle. You know there's a stream flowing out of it, though. Take a conservative bearing downstream. Simple. You could manage this without a compass if you had to, but hitting the pond in the middle without a compass would be pure dumb luck. If you want to retrace your steps to the top of the rise from the pond, you follow a back bearing. It's simple. Let's say that the course you walked on the way out was 78°. Add half a circle to that figure, or 180°, giving you a bearing of 258° to follow. If your original bearing was more than 180°, subtract 180° from it. If you walked out on a bearing of 210°, subtract half a circle and you have a thirty-degree bearing to walk back. Use the same treesight technique and you'll be back on the ridge in no time.

This is fine—unless you find a healthy swamp barring your way between the ridge and the pond. You could slog on through it or across it, but there's an easier way. You know from observation and from the contour lines on the map that the valley you're traversing tilts downhill, as it were, to your left. Try the high side of the swamp for easier passage. You're walking a bearing of 78° already, so you'll make a 90° turn to your right. Your bearing is now 78 plus 90, or 168°. Sight against some prominent landmark and start walking. But this time, count every double step you take, and jot the number down in your little notebook. Go far enough to clear the obstacle. Turn left 90°, which puts you back on your original bearing, and walk that until you're sure you're across the swamp. Then turn left. For this, you'll subtract 90° from your original bearing of 78°, and you'll walk a bearing of 348°. Zero and 360 are coincident. No problem. Think of it as minus twelve, if you wish—as long as the direction of travel arrow and 348° are lined up, and the magnetic needle is oriented with the orienting arrow.

Here's the tricky part. When you first turned right off your original course, you walked 350 double steps. When you turned left, to "cross" the swamp, how far you traveled didn't matter. But this left turn will take you back to the original line you were following—and the best way to get there, short of carrying a surveyor's chain, is to walk that same 350 double steps along that 348° heading. When you've done that, turn right again, reorient your compass, take a field bearing of 78° and march boldly on, smiling the smug smirk of the newly informed.

I suppose you're wondering why you just can't march across that swamp in winter. After all, it's covered with snow, isn't it? Yep, it is. And underneath that snow may be solid ice, or open water, or slush, or more commonly, a random mixture of all three. I'll gladly march an extra half mile to avoid wet feet in summer—and I'll extend that to a fair number of miles in winter. The reason is obvious if I've done my job earlier. In case I haven't, wet feet and wet clothing in cold weather are open invitations to nearly instant frostbite and hypothermia. Keeping your powder dry is small consolation if the rest of you is wet at -10°F!

Some common—or uncommon—sense has to be called into play here, of course. A ski pole or an ice axe can serve as a prod in uneasy terrain. Also, some awareness of weather patterns is helpful. A cold and relatively snowless early winter will generally freeze most open water that isn't moving at a brisk pace or disturbed by spring holes. On the other hand, a warm autumn followed by a heavy early snow may keep waterways relatively open underneath the snow blanket for the whole winter, or at least until the January thaw and freeze cycle is completed. This is a common occurrence in some areas, notable among them Minnesota's Boundary Waters Canoe Area.

Another point, while we're at it. If you're running a field bearing, don't blithely assume that you can forget the backbearing and simply follow your tracks out. In heavily wooded areas, chances are that you can. But even "chances are" doesn't imply *certainty*, and all veteran winter freaks have seen days when a heavy snow and a brisk wind have covered up a well-defined trail broken out by four snowshoers a mere two hours before. In open terrain, or on open summits, the process can take two minutes.

There are cogent reasons for restricting your travel to out-and-back trips until you grow accustomed to winter travel and navigation. A loop trip implies that you're committed to completion, and you'll often get deked into gutting out the loop in adverse conditions when it would be easier to retrace your steps, even if the miles covered are longer.

Let's look at an example from my backyard. There's a ridge system out there paralleling the Mohawk River, and the total vertical ascent is about 1200 feet. One of our favorite time-killers in winter is a trip up the mountain on an old ski trail to where it intersects with a powerline complex that runs the ridge. We then turn right and follow the ridge until it intersects an abandoned downhill ski trail after two miles or so. We then lope down the trail, turn right again and follow a maze of tote roads back to the base of the mountain. Wilderness it isn't—but the ridge is exposed, windy and subject to some imposing drifts up where it intersects with the old ski area trails. If the weather turns bad en route, it's easier walking or skiing to turn around on the ridge and retrace our trail than it is to slug out the half mile or so of exposed ridge to get to the ski trail and a "shorter" way back. Winter trips are measured in energy expenditure rather than in miles. It is far less tiring to retrace a trail than to break a new one—and your route finding has been done for you. The lesson is simple. Remember thy backbearing and use it until you're very secure in the winter forests—and even then, don't take beginners on loop trips unless you've done them before yourself and **know** that they'll "go."

Yeah, I'm being a middleaged fussbudget. I know. But I'm out there to have a good time; I'm not out there to prove something. Not any more. Time was . . . but that's a part of the learning process. Back to maps!

Working from a map is totally different. You don't have to worry about declination, that difference between true north and magnetic north, when you're following a field bearing, but you do when you're working from a map. If the declination is small, say one degree or thereabouts, you can forget about it unless you're a true map and compass freak, but the 14° declination you face in the Adirondacks is considerable. In fact, it can mean about a quarter-mile error for each mile of travel, which is an imposing chunk of territory. There are two ways to handle declination. The first, and most commonly used, is as follows:

Place the compass on the map so that the long edge of the compass board connects the two points between which you want to travel. Next, rotate the bezel of the compass until the orienting arrow (NOT the needle—the orienting arrow) is pointing true north. On USGS sheets, this is parallel to the side of the map. Your bearing will be where the direction of travel arrow intersects the compass housing. Note that figure. If you were walking a simple field bearing, that would be it.

But to compensate for declination, you have to add or subtract the degrees of declination from your bearing. In the Adirondacks, that's roughly 14° west. In fact, until you get into Florida, central and western Tennessee, and western Kentucky, your eastern maps will always show a west declination. If the declination is west, add it to your field bearing. If it's east, subtract it. There's an old rhyme that will help you remember that—East is least, and West is best.

I've always thought of that as the hard way to do it. I correct my maps before I use them. Here's how. Remember that declination arrow? Take a straightedge and extend that line all the way across the map with a pencil or a ball point. Then use your straightedge to draw parallel lines to it covering the map.

With these lines drawn, life is simpler. Connect the two points you wish to travel between with your compass base plate, swing the bezel until the orienting arrow is parallel with one of the magnetic north lines you've drawn, and read your bearing where the direction of travel arrow intersects the bezel. This way you don't have to correct for declination.

I'd like to think that it was all this simple, but it never turns out to be. Here's a common example. You've parked your car along an unfamiliar dirt road running sort of east-west to scramble through some hackberry to an attractive little hill about a mile and a half off the road. There isn't a trail, and you don't have a map, but your faithful Polaris is sitting in your daybag. Great. You can see the hill from the road, and your field bearing is exactly due north. Off you go, following the landmark to landmark procedure we've talked about. In a bit less than two hours, you're on top of the hill, and the view is certainly pretty. It was worth the sweat.

Later, you head on back to the car. It's a simple enough back bearing. Due south. In due time you arrive at the road. Hmmm. No car. Oh, well, should be just up the road a piece. Dunno. This doesn't look familiar. Maybe it's down the road a piece. Damn. Which way is it? Off you go, up the road. After a half mile or more, you're convinced it isn't that way, so you turn around. It starts to rain. You burrow into your daybag for your poncho and, oh my, that's right, the kids took it to camp. Ouch. Back down the road at a fast trot as the skies open up. Around the corner from where you came out of the woods is your car. You climb in, drenched and muttering imprecations. "Damn compass is wrong. Damn that Roberts guy. He didn't tell me the right things to do! Mumble. Grizzle, grouse, grouse, DAMN!" To top it off, your matches are wet and you don't even have the solace of a pipeful of tobacco.

Well, you've been had by the commonest mistake of the novice map and compass freak. Take this as solace. The error here is easy to spot. Unless you're incredibly meticulous, and use a very accurate sighting compass like a Suunto or a Brunton, you're not going to be able to run a bearing much closer than one degree. This isn't much of an error, but it's enough to confuse you with roads and streams. The solution is equally evident. Instead of running a due south back bearing, run a bearing of maybe 185 degrees. No, you won't arrive at your car, but you're certain that you'll arrive on the road somewhere a bit to the west of your car. Then it's simple. Turn left at the road, and you'll find your car.

This is all well and good. You know how to follow a compass bearing, how to develop one from a map and follow it, and how to establish a base line, which is the fancy name for finding your way back to the car parked along the road. What happens if you've been wandering about without following your compass and you'd like to know where you are? If you have a map, the compass will help. If you don't it will help you get out of trouble, but it can't tell you where you are. First the map.

You've dropped off the trail and headed up the side of a knob that you thought was a satellite peak to a mountain you wanted to climb, but you've been charging along now for some time, and you have that distinctly uneasy feeling that you're not where you think you are. No trouble, but inconvenient and embarrassing. You know where you are well enough to beat back down the hill and pick up the trail that runs along its foot, but that's a long way. Off in the distance, you spot two prominent peaks and a lot of smaller ones. You recognize one of them, and it's fairly easy to determine what the other one is from the map. You now have two known points to work from, and you have your map out and oriented. Take a back bearing of one peak. Sight against the direction of travel arrow on your compass and turn the housing until the north part of the needle is in line with the orienting arrow. Now you have the magnetic back bearing, which you read off the bezel where the direction of travel arrow intersects it. Now put the compass on the map, with one back corner touching the peak. Swing the base plate, using the peak as the axis of rotation, until the orienting arrow is parallel to a magnetic north-south line. Draw a line along the edge of the compass. You're somewhere along this line. In some situations, that one point would be enough for you to have a fair idea of your location, especially if the landmarks of the area are prominent. If you're really confused, you need to take the backbearing of the other peak you recognized in the distance, and do the same thing. After you've drawn your second line, you'll note that the lines cross. You are sitting where the lines cross.

The first clear day you get, take your map and compass out in the field and practice with them. Learn to orient the compass and the map, learn to follow field bearings and back bearings, practice walking from and returning to a base line, and try your hand at resection in known territory. Take this book along, if you think you'll need it. Take a friend along, too. It may help if the friend knows compass work, but if he doesn't, you can both learn together. And take a relaxed, easy head.

One afternoon fiddling with a compass in a more or less organized way will tell you everything you'll ever need to find your way. If your chosen area has a hill with a good view, you'll find out a lot about those lines and symbols on the map as well. Most of them are evident. The broken line symbol indicates a trail. This doesn't mean that the trail's still there, of course. If the date of the map in the lower right hand corner is fairly recent, it may be. If it's an oldie, don't depend on it. Don't depend on finding all the unimproved roads indicated by a double row of broken lines, either, although a little judicious woodcraft and poking around will enable you to find a log road that's been unused for fifty years and covered with underbrush.

The only markings on a top sheet that might not be self-explanatory are those miserable wiggly brown lines running all over the place. They're called *contour lines*, because they form a picture of what the contours of the terrain look like. The theory is simple. A contour line is an imaginary line on the ground along which the elevation above sea level is constant. Sometimes another base is used, but don't sweat it. The difference in elevation between contour lines is called *contour interval*, and it appears on the bottom margin of the map, in the center, right under the scales. It's typically twenty feet on the 15 minute maps and ten feet on the 7½ minute maps. The heavy lines indicate 100 foot intervals, while the thin lines are as stated on the map. If you follow one of the heavy lines long enough, you'll probably find a number on it, usually in brown print. This is the elevation, and the brown print tells you that it is calculated from aerial photographs by photogrammetric methods. Figures in black have been verified in the field. If you look at the contour lines of a familiar ridge while you're looking at the ridge itself, you'll soon see how they work. So much for the difficulties of map and compass work.

Getting lost in winter is potentially a lot more hazardous than wandering astray in summer—which is all the more reason for making sure of your map and compass skills before you need them. But what happens if you get lost? Nothing—if you have your program assembled. You can retrace your route. You have the advantages of visibility and ubiquitous shelter. You have, of course, the necessary living items in your pack. And somebody—preferably several somebodies—knows where you were going and when you expected to return. If you can't retrace your route due to snowfall or nightfall, dig in, make yourself comfortable, and relax and enjoy it. With the advent of a new day, you may be able to pick up your route and backtrack. At the very least, you'll be able to locate your position on a map, and either move out in an obvious direction (like a backtrack) or stay put. If you're prepared, you have no cause for concern. Even if you're less well prepared than you might be, an easy mind and a relaxed spirit are worth any amount of emergency rations. Sure, it's colder out there—but there ain't no damn black flies! □

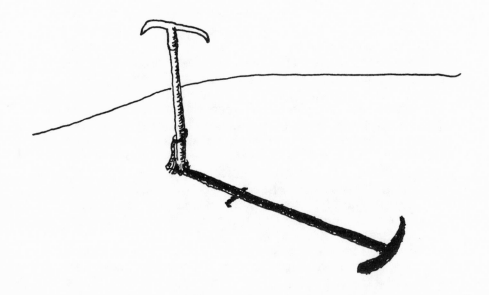

WINTER TRIP ORGANIZATION

All winter hiking beyond a casual ramble in the south woodlot is predicated, for better or worse, on one idea: "There ain't no Ski Patrol out there." A winter hiking party is its own best friend, counselor, medical technician, weather forecaster and guide. Accordingly, each member has to submerge the extremes of his or her free spirit to keep the group functioning smoothly and safely. I almost regret having to say this, because I'm not always the most sedate, easily regimented soul in the universe myself. It's not a question, really, of regimentation; it's a question of acceptance of responsibility for your own actions and a recognition that your actions can enhance or endanger the group you're with.

Obviously, there's a difference in preparation level for an overnight (or longer) trip, a hard day trip in remote terrain, and an all-day jaunt on snowshoes or skis that, however many miles you may cover, takes you no further than a half-mile from civilization. Preparations for the latter are obvious. Preparations for the hard day trip and the overnights are rather more complex. Let's look at the tough ones and work down from them.

To begin with, a winter party is just that—a party. The hardcore winter freaks are pretty much in agreement that a party requires four people. The reasoning is straightforward. In the event of an unfortunate incident, one person can stay with the injured party and two can go for help, assuming that the route itself is potentially hazardous. Under winter conditions, an injury like a severe ankle sprain can be potentially fatal if it renders the victim unable to provide for shelter and warmth. In other words, all routes in remote country in winter are to be considered hazardous, and should not be attempted alone except in dire emergency.

If I knew the folks with whom I was hiking really well, I'd certainly consider a smaller party for, say, an easy flatland trek. But for something that could be pretty grim in the event of bad weather, like a winter ascent of Kathadin or a traverse of the Presidential Range or the Great Range, four would be a minimum.

It's obvious that any hiking party, in winter or summer, moves at the pace of its slowest member and covers the distance that its weakest member can cover. If you're a barn-burner, go hike with other barnburners. Don't hike with me. I'm slow. I can be slow for sixteen hours in a row and more if I have to, but I'm not a trail runner. I'm a gangly knot of very slow-twitch muscle fiber that starts to warm up to the task about suppertime. I hate to get up early, too—and I dearly love to walk at night. In winter, of course, it's particularly easy if there's a sliver of a moon and good snow cover. The point is that a party for a rough trip should be selected on the basis of compatibility of "style" as well as friendship, unless you're all willing to make concessions without feeling virtuously long-suffering. You can, of course, make some intelligent adap-tations. I'll break trail all through the shank of the day and be a regular Mary Poppins around camp if you're willing to do most of the morning work. For some folks, this is fine. Three of our current household are morning people. The eight-year-old and I are helpless blobs of protoplasm in the early hours. On the trail, we get poured into our skis by the others. Long about early afternoon, Old Greeneyes and Daddy come on like gangbusters, and by five o'clock, I'm ready to *break* trail until midnight.

I say **we** worked it out, and **we** did. All of us. I suppose that I'm the nominal leader of our family expeditions, but the real leader is the person who's most tired, or the slowest. And that's how any group has to be "led." If you ever have the op-portunity to take a group of beginners out for a pleasant day's jaunt in your friendly local state forest, don't, please don't, play Hero Mountaineer And Intrepid Leader. Play Trepid Leader. Don't push the weakest member of your party into exhaustation! Fib a little if you have to. Create an old soccer injury or something—but keep the party together physically and emotionally. It's probably worse to be an obvious Patient Sufferer than it is to be a martinet who yells, "C'mon, Charlie, get your butt in gear!" all the time, but neither attitude becomes a trip leader who's dealing with novices.

This brings up the question of whether there should be a trip leader at all. Obviously, a clutch of novices can benefit immensely from subtle, low-key, competent leadership. An experienced party may well adopt a consensus, as long as all the members agree beforehand that major decisions such as how much farther to go or when to turn back must be un-animous. Of course, an experienced party of good friends who've wandered together a lot develops a *primus inter pares* leadership that may vary from situation to situation. Some folks blow sky high if they don't see a trail marker every fifty feet; I'm a happy, confident bushwhacker—although my routes are rather roundabout at times.

However, on any trip that goes beyond the south forty, it's best to designate a leader or devise a system to take care of the leader's functions in one critical area—that of responsibility for party emergency gear.

The winter party, again, **must** be a self-contained, self-sufficient unit. This means that a day-tripping party in anything resembling remote terrain must be prepared to stay out overnight if necessary, and to provide warmth and shelter for an injured hiker. This doesn't mean that everybody goes equipped with sleeping bags and that the party carries a tent. It does mean, though, that everybody goes equipped with a small nylon tarp or groundcloth and an insulated jacket, and that the leader carries a sleeping bag, a closed-cell foam pad, a stove and pot, emergency rations, and extra matches and firestarter packed in a sealed container. I like a plastic bottle with grey boat tape to seal the cap, myself. The sleeping bag and foam pad are for an injured or hypothermic member of the party, and the stove, food and matches are pretty self-explanatory. It's assumed that each member has his or her own food for the day, and matches stashed in several spots, but one person (call him or her the leader, if you will) is responsible for this other gear. The leader may not have to tote it; in this situation, the gear can be distributed—but somebody **must** be responsible for its presence. I hope this doesn't sound like nagging or like I'm trying to impose some quasi-military organization on a simple trek in the boonies. I'm not. I just feel that if you're going out there to have a good time, it makes sense to take that little extra with you to insure that you have a safe time as well. □

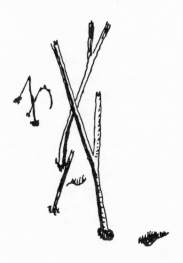

WHAT TO TAKE—
AND NOT TO TAKE

We've talked a lot about equipment, and even more about how to use it. We've even talked about what to bring— and not to bring—in general terms. Let's look at something more specific now. I'm going to pull a couple of packs off the shelf in the closet and start stuffing things in them. Everything but food—except for that one small parcel of emergency ration that goes with me everywhere and is **never** broken into except on the trail in an emergency.

Let's start with a simple, easy two-hour walk on snowshoes up the back hill. I might not bother to pack anything at all for this—but let's assume it's a pretty cold day. I'll wear my usual outfit—long johns, GI wool pants and wind-pants, wool socks, shoepacs, net shirt, wool shirt, parka, balaclava, and mittens. Spare mittens go into the pack. So does a lighter weight wool hat (my nightcap). Matches and firestarter live in a sealed tin in the pack. I'll take the compass and the map packet just to set a good example; for this trip, I don't need them. But I do need the matches and firestarter. And I need my pocket knife, a razor-sharp little Schrade. The emergency food pack also goes in. It's ridiculous, I suppose, but I could break a leg up there and the food might be a solace if not a necessity. Next item is a down vest. It's a dry, cold day; otherwise I'd take a synthetic vest. I have lots of room in the pack, so I stuff the vest into a rather large sack (out of kindness to the down). Then I'll fill a waterbottle with warm water from the faucet, wrap my Sit-Upon around it, and toss that into the pack. If I felt really hedonistic, I might fill up a vacuum bottle with coffee, tea or cocoa. A pound more or less on this jaunt is meaningless. I'd also throw in my little aluminized Mylar emergency "space blanket"—again, more out of habit than necessity—and a short chunk of parachute cord in case a binding gives up the ghost. I'd put my sunglasses in my parka pocket, drop a few hard candies in another pocket, and take off.

It's obvious that I've taken more than I needed for a short jaunt on turf that I can walk—and ski—on a moonless night. But I'm covered against any untoward event, and I've maintained the habit of bringing certain things. Oddly enough, I'd take less if Molly and the boys were going, because there'd be no real problem then in case of a sprain or some such incident. Besides, I have a new compass, a Suunto RA-69 DE, with a "pace memorizer" that Orienteering competitors use, and it's a great toy. It's even more fun than the clinometer on my old Silva Ranger!

I'd like to note in passing that a quick little ramble like this is an excellent time to fuss around with a map and a compass. It's fun, and it's a good way to hone your skills to a level that gives you the confidence to find your way in any situation. It's also a good time to introduce novices to the so-called "mysteries" of map and compass work. Somehow you learn better when you can see the results and feel them through your bootsoles!

Let's take a longer day trip next. This one's going to be in more demanding terrain, and we'll be out for most of the day. We'll be on snowshoes this time, too, and there'll be four in the party—two adults and two youngsters. This imposes some additional thought and preparation. The kids are strong. They're little knotty bundles of cardiovascular energy. But they can't carry much, and they require almost constant infusions of food. They can, however, carry their extra clothing and a water bottle—but Daddy and Mommy cheat a bit and carry *extra* extra socks and mittens for them.

I need a bigger pack for this sort of trip. I have a small teardrop pack that I use for random scoots around home, but "my" middle-sized rucksack—an old Alp Eiger that's really been through the wars—is Molly's, and she'll be carrying it today. I'll carry my big Synergy Works subframed bag, which is more than I need, but it's what I got. It's big enough that I don't have to fool around stuffing jackets into tiny, tiny stuffsacks, though.

The obvious things get packed first. Emergency rations, matches and firestarter, spare hat, mittens and socks plus spares for the boys, our "regular" food (pocket munchies gc with each hiker), waterbottle, teapot, small stove, Sit-Upon, and a small bottle of extra fuel for the stove. I'll hike in the same garb that I'd use around home, but I'll stuff a big *Polarguard* parka into the pack for extra insulation at lunch. It's more than necessary, but it's warm enough for a bivouac if it should be necessary. In the bottom compartment goes a sleeping bag, bivvy cover and closed-cell foam pad—just in case. I also roll up an 8 x 10 nylon tarp in a stuff sack along with some parachute cord. I like a reasonable degree of comfort on the trail—and if it's windy, I can erect a windbreak with the tarp in two shakes. I'll pack my shovel, too. It might be a good day to show the boys how to do a trench shelter. I've shown them before, but it never hurts to show them again.

The map goes into the header of Molly's Eiger today. The compass lives in the pocket of my wool shirt, and is secured to the buttonhole by a lanyard. Molly and the boys all carry whistles. I should also but I don't. Never have—and don't plan to. Obstinate—and foolish. Molly also carries her compass. We're in country we know well; if we weren't, we'd both have maps in case an emergency forced us to split the party.

There are hazards in winter; more possibilities with kids along. There are also hazards in summer hiking as well as canoeing. We've never "trained" our kids, except in the fundamentals of canoe safety. We just take them along a lot and let them experience the world. I've never been a believer in that type of indoctrination that some folks subject kids to; the outdoors should be **fun**—first, last and always. You can talk from now until Hell freezes over about spiritual and esthetic values, but if you weren't having direct physical *fun* tromping around in the outback, you wouldn't be out there!

Kids can function well on a winter trip if you've taken them out enough so that they have confidence in themselves and give you confidence in them. I'll confess that we've gotten more than a little annoyed when the lads come in to the kitchen from a winter afternoon and the older one, age nine, tells us that the old downhill area trails up the ridge were a real gas, or when they come marching in from a summer night soaking wet to tell us that they buried the Jensen racing canoe trying to surf the wake of a 60 foot cabin cruiser on the Mohawk. But I think we'd be more annoyed if they planted their rumps on the sofa and soaked up TV every afternoon. So—we take our kids on winter trips. And on canoe trips. And they take themselves. Plato was wrong. Experience is, ultimately, the **only** teacher.

Back to the pack. On a long, hard daytrip, I may well be tempted to carry an extra string shirt and either a light sweater or an old G.I. undershirt, the kind that unbuttons partway down the front. If it's particularly cold (and I may need more insulation) or particularly warm (and I'll sweat heavily in spite of myself), I'll most likely take both. The pleasant, calm winter day that starts at 10°F in the morning and goes up to 25°F in the mid-afternoon offers the least problem as far as clothing goes.

For an overnight or a weekend, I don't really need anything more except food. But because I like my luxury, I'd take a tent. I would naturally take the tent if the family was going. We're not there to rough it; we're there to smooth it! I'd also take my candle lantern and candles for some cheer around the campsite, and my sleeping bag array may be modified depending on the nature of the trip and the weather. I'll also find room for an extra pair of liners for my shoepacs—if I'm wearing shoepacs—and I'll certainly carry a pair of mukluks for use around camp and in the tent. My mukluks are fleshed out with felt shoepac liners, so I don't need to tote anything "extra" for them.

The nature of any particular trip, or the mode of travel I choose, may alter some peripherals that I carry. Obviously, a ski tour requires at least a minimum of waxes and some spare dingbats for skis and bindings. A peakbagging trip will require creepers for the snowshoes and an ice axe, and most probably the big, uncomfortable Mickey Mouse boots and a pair of crampons. I may eschew the latter, however, if it's a family trip, because none of us are strongly motivated to "get the peak." I was at one time, but I've learned from Molly and the kids, who've always understood that the journey itself is more important than the destination.

This may seem to be a strange attitude for a family that competes occasionally in citizen's races on cross-country skis and competes avidly in canoe races, but it isn't. The race is run stride by stride, stroke by stroke, each performed as well as possible with no thought for the one before and none for the one ahead. We walk that way, too, savoring the moment, without concern for the destination. As you read this, note that the most important breath you'll ever draw is the one you're drawing NOW. And you can say the same for each step in a journey of a million steps!

Oh yes—sometimes we don't pack our packs at all. We throw everything into a little Norwegian-made fiberglass sled (*fjellpulk* in Norsk) that we used years ago to tow the kids around in while we skied—and I must concede that forty pounds on a *pulk* is a helluva lot easier to manage than forty pounds in the best pack in the world. There are some problems, of course. Skiing down a long, fast hill is interesting, to say the least, and heaving the thing up a steep, short pitch is just pure and simple grunt work, but it's a most pleasant way to travel on either skis or snowshoes if the terrain is at all forgiving. Someday, my buddy Dave Clayman and I will get around to training his husky bitch, Shakti, to the *pulk*, and some winter trips at least will be nothing but fat city! Some day. Meanwhile, I'm not planning to throw away my big pack!

Whoops! Wait a second. Somebody out there's saying, "Hey, Harry, you take more than this! No first aid kit? No knife? No sunglasses? No toilet paper, even?" Well, yes—but I figure that there are some things you don't need to be reminded of—like toilet paper. But maybe I'm wrong. Regarding this inelegant, if vital, commodity, the best route is to provide each party member with a personal supply and keep some in reserve just in case. Ziplok bags are appropriate storage containers.

Don't, by the way, feel that a blanket of snow is an open invitation to random elimination. The river's still there, whether you can see it or not—and it will survive nicely without your e *coli*, thank you. Find a thicket sheltered from the wind and make that the camp latrine. And burn your toilet paper, please. Thanks.

First aid kits? Sure, I carry one, but I'm always hesitant to tell you what to take, at least past aspirin, adhesive bandages, an ankle wrap, a triangular bandage and some soap. I may embellish the kit with an intestinal tranquilizer, a pain-killer, a muscle relaxant and a broad-spectrum antibiotic for long trips, and I'll usually take the pain-killer and the muscle relaxant on a hard day trip, where a back spasm or a painfully wrenched knee could pose a problem. I don't have the need for any regular medication. If I did, I'd be absolutely certain it was in the pack, and if it could withstand long-term storage, some of it would be in the emergency ration too! The same with eyeglasses. I need them to read, but I can function without them on a wilderness trip if I have to, so I don't take a spare pair. My buddy Dave, though, literally can't find his glasses in our kitchen if he has to take them off for some reason and they're moved out of reach. He carries a spare pair—and uses a Glass-Gard all the time. If you walk into trees without your glasses, pack a spare pair.

Sunglasses—actually, glacier glasses—live in my parka in a case, which in turn lives in a small stuff bag that contains a stick of lip salve (usually Bonne Bell, because it tastes good), a tube of Glacier Creme for my nose and cheekbones, both of which are prominent, and a tube of a German lip salve for high-elevation protection called Labiosan. It burns, tastes like dead socks, and is expensive. It works.

My little pocket knife lives in my pocket. Molly's big Swiss Army knife lives in her pocket. Mine is in a small leather bag that's attached to a belt loop with a thin cord. Her knife has a lanyard ring, and it's secured to her with a cord and a big snap swivel. I also keep a sharpening stone in the knife bag, because I'm a terrible fussbudget about knives. A sharp one is a useful tool; a dull one is both useless and dangerous.

I carry an old Taylor thermometer in my shirt pocket, a delightful toy and a scientifically valid means of collecting data for later boasting. "Cold? Man, my thermometer read minus twenty-seven in the morning!" I carry innumerable boxes of Coghlan's waterproof matches in my pack, in my parka, in my shirt, in my pants, and occasionally in the rolled-up part of my Balaclava. (They're easy to reach there when I light the stove and my pipe at mug-up.) This is in addition to the emergency supply that's never used except when the regular supply is dead. And I carry a light. Up until now, it's been a little Mallory with alkaline cells in it, but John Fitzgerald, *Wilderness Camping's* publisher, has been extolling the virtues of MSR's lithium cell conversion for the Justrite headlamp, and he's convinced me. Guess I'll have to try one. The lithium "battery" loses little, if any, oomph in cold weather. While it's expensive initially, it's very long lived and a good value.

My cooking gear contains within its innards the K.P. stuff—a biodegradable detergent (either Campsuds or Sutter's), a Dobie, and one of those paper cleaning cloths that seems to last forever.

Now—down to the nitty and the gritty. Most of the questions I've received about *Movin' Out* were about specific items of equipment—chiefly of the "what do you use and why" variety. I've been less specific in this book, chiefly because I feel strongly that you should use what you have and what your experience has told you will do the job **for you.** Also, there's a lot of equipment in this house. We have a large family, some of whom are away either in school or working, and some of their gear is here because we're convenient to the mountains. At times we try out prototype gear from various manufacturers. What we use regularly, though—in other words what we grab when there's no gear we have to test—is apt to vary a lot.

Some gear is predictable. Molly uses her old Alp Eiger as both a daybag and a medium-sized rucksack for longer trips, and I think it would follow her out of the house by itself if she forgot it. It's also her carry-on luggage when she flies. My "pet" daybag is a well-used Sierra Designs Daytripper, and I'll sometimes augment that with a fanny pack of unknown origins. If I need to tote a lot, I'll either use my D4 Jan Sport frame pack or (more and more lately and all the time when I'm skiing) my big Synergy Work subframe pack. Why the Jan Sport? It fits me and is comfortable. Why the Synergy Works sack? Like the Jan Sport, it fits me. I'm also absolutely taken with the workmanship of the thing. It looks right, works, fits, and is made impeccably. At the risk of offending some good friends who make some fine, fine subframe packs for a lot less money, the Synergy pack is simply the best in the world. In truth, it's better than I'll ever need—and it was a monstrous extravagance—but I'd do it again, so help me. Molly uses her Alp Expedition bag and frame most of the time for heavy going; for light overnights and weekends, she uses a Kelty Ski Tour. I don't have to slap her hands when she paws covetously at my pack—it doesn't fit her! The Kelty does, and she likes the way it follows her movements.

I have no strong preferences among our sleeping bags. Molly goes with her Camp 7 North Col winter and summer, using it inside a *Polarguard* mummy for really bitter weather.

I'm a faithful user of my old Optimus 111 B stove on all winter trips. The backup stove varies. The new Coleman is good, as is the big Phoebus. The MSR stoves, both the white gas and the multifuel models, are superb performers. Why, then, do I take my 111 B? Because I've taken it for years and years and know all its quirks and vagaries. Big Blue Box and I came to an understanding years and years ago. I give it affection; it gives me flame. And neither of us have broken that compact.

About the only other things we're devoted to are our mountain parkas. Molly's is a Sierra West Storm King, a Gore-Tex coat, or a Camp 7 Venture Cloth one, depending on the weather. Mine depends on whim, but they're both Synergy Works coats. One's a five-layer Ventile jobbie that I once called "the best damn parka in the world" in a review in *Wilderness Camping;* subsequent experience with it has only confirmed that opinion. The other is a Whitewater parka in *Gore-Tex*. If it looks like wet snow or rain, the *Gore-Tex* coat wins. If it's just plain cold, so cold your fillings ache, the Ventile coat gets the nod.

There are always some quirky items that you've used so long that you never question. One of mine is a red wool Troll hat that I use as a nightcap. I have a blue Troll hat too, but the red one is my nightcap. It may be my day cap as well—but it's **always** my nightcap. It feels warmer than the blue one. And I have a pair of woolen mittens, **double** mittens, made in Johnstown, New York, but I've never been able to find out by whom, that are the greatest thing since sliced bread. They always go with me. Molly has a down vest that a friend of ours, Nancy Pytlak, made some years ago that always is in her pack or on her bod, winter or summer. Generally, though, she has fewer quirks about gear than I have. She'd use the MSR stove all the time, for example, if it was up to her. But I'm the cook, so it isn't. And I'll use wooden snowshoes except when I have to use my little Sherpas for steep work. Molly used a pair of Early Winters Northern Lights shoes last year and hasn't even nodded at our wooden snowshoes since then, although she did help me varnish them.

If you learn nothing else from this ramble, I hope you learned that you should absolutely trust no man's (or woman's) opinion regarding the gear that **you** have to live with. General principles? Fine. Nightcaps are great, and there's a sound measurable reason for them. But between ourselves, a blue one's just as warm as a red one. For you. Not for me! □

BACKPACK ON SKIS

The cross-country ski is more than transportation; it's a sensual delight that wakes up every muscle fiber, every frayed little nerve ending. Unfortunately, most ski tourers find that backpacking on skis is far from the exhilarating pastime they're programmed to expect. In deep, untracked snow or in steep, knotty terrain, the touring ski simply isn't as efficient an instrument as the snowshoe, unless it's being wielded by somebody who's considered the problems beforehand and taken pains to solve them.

It's not the obvious problems that do in the casual tourer who decides to spend a weekend on skis rather than on snowshoes. True; deep, unpacked snow is a hassle, but it's a hassle on snowshoes, too—and a party of four or more can break out a satisfactory trail with either skis or snowshoes. If you're not running a loop route—and you shouldn't be—you can ski back on a broken trail with some pleasure. It's no more difficult breaking trail with skis than with snowshoes (plenty of hard work either way!), but the technique for breaking trail with skis is less obvious, and requires a modicum of skiing skills. More on this later.

You'll find it easier to wend your frustrated way through big boulders and up short, nearly vertical "steps" on snowshoes. And the snowshoe's advantage in puckerbrush requires little embellishment by me. Being forced to back and fill and pull your ski tips out from under branches every third step is no fun! To solve this, just don't ski in pucker-brush. Don't plan a trip that commits you to endless miles of boulder gardens, hitchy-bops, spruce thickets and tag alder! You can cope with short stretches of this dismal stuff. You can even pack snowshoes with you to cope with these patches if you choose. But it's simpler to select a skiing route that's more adapted to the requirements that the ski—and skiing—impose.

Now let's take another look at trail-breaking on skis. Even the perfect ski route can, at times, be hip-deep in fresh powder. In some areas, it'll consolidate quickly, but never as quickly as you'd like. You might as well learn to cope with it. Recognize that really deep, fluffy snow is a most uncommon occurrence outside of the high country. Heavy snowfalls in the East are generally the products of either a storm coming off the Great Lakes, where a warm air mass from the Ohio Valley has collided with a slug of Canadian air, or the classic coastal storm. The storms off the lakes generally ride the crest of some brisk winds, which toss and consolidate (and drift!) the snow; the coastal storms generally deposit a fairly wet snow that's hard to slog through when it's fresh, but firms up nicely in a day or so. The deep, fluffy stuff in the high country and the Northern Plains, while intimidating to the novice, is, well, *fluffy,* and you can kick through 18 inches of Colorado champagne powder with a lot less effort than you can move through six inches of fresh concrete snow in the Jersey Pine Barrens. Then there's that Eastern and Midwestern phenomenon called "breakable crust" for which the best technique is to stay home.

Breaking trail—or skiing in unbroken snow that's not so deep as to reduce you to slogging—requires rethinking your equipment a bit. It doesn't, surprisingly, require a wide ski of the kind generally referred to as a "touring ski." The wide ski will give you a little more lateral stability in deep snow, but it won't buy you more floatation. That's because the tip and shovel of the wider ski are stiffer, and like to "dive" under the snow rather than float over it. If you have wide skis, fine. Use them. If you scoot around the neighborhood and take day trips on so-called "light touring skis" like most tourers do, that's fine, too. They work. They've worked for me for years— in the Adirondacks, in the Whites, in the Rockies, in all kinds of snow, and with heavy packs. But. . . I didn't use my low-cut, superlight running boots, and after one dismal trip, I substituted a big subframe rucksack for my frame pack. No, I'm not crazy. My friend Ned Gillette has done some insanely demanding Arctic trips—Alaska's Brooks Range and Ellesmere Island among them—on light touring skis, and while Ned is, conservatively, 18 times better on skis than I am, the trips he's done are probably 18 times tougher than any of mine, so I calculate that our experiences are equal in terms of informing you that you *can* backpack on skinny skis.

Why the sturdier boot? For warmth? Yes, but only partly. A little creativity or a few bucks invested in polyester-insulated or foam-insulated overboots (I use a pair made by Lowe Alpine Systems and I'm most happy with them) will keep your feet warm even if you're wearing racing boots. You need the sturdier boot to control the ski on the relatively unstable platform that deep snow offers. This doesn't mean that the bootsole has to be stiff as a board fore and aft. It has to be stiff *in torsion,* so the ski doesn't roll, pitch, yaw, dive, rock, roll and plunge under you, and so you can extract the ski tip from a thorn thicket without having the bootsole tie itself in knots. Your boot should also be higher than the low-cut running boot. Frankly, you get precious little "ankle support" from most touring boots, unless you go to the very high-topped ones. Even then, those midcalf-length tops are either of soft, soft leather or fabric, and intended more as gaiters than as "support." Truly supportive boots would eat holes in your Achilles tendons in no time. What you need is a boot that's high enough to keep your heel firmly in place even if your ankle rolls over a little bit.

The boot must obviously be sturdy. This is no place to fool around with synthetic uppers and a cheap sole with no reinforcement around the binding pin holes. For years, the Eastern tourer has rooted around in the big Alfa touring boots or Fabiano touring boots, but the last few years have seen new entries in the marketplace to challenge these old favorites of the backwoods crowd. In the early days of touring, before the boom began, most gear was oriented toward the backwoods skier or the racer. As the sport became popular, the middle of the bell curve was filled in quickly, and while racing gear never dropped out of sight completely, the backwoods skier, who was by then a small part of the market, was neglected by most importers. The sport's still growing, and I hope it grows until every American in the snow belt is on skis, although I appreciate that this idea may be anathema to some folks. The solution to crowded trails is not to restrict the practice of the sport—it's to develop more trails!

Along with the continued growth of touring has come a new market for backwoods touring gear, especially boots. The "new" tourer enjoys the golf course, the touring center's groomed trails, and the outback as well. You can be sure that if a market exists for sturdy touring boots, somebody will rush to fill it. The market exists—and the boots are there. They never vanished in the Scandinavian market, but few importers were willing to risk bringing them in in any quantity and even fewer retailers would handle them. Would you carry a decent distribution of an Alfa touring boot that retailed for $50 at a time when your customers were hassling you because they could buy a cheap, made-in-Formosa boot

123

with synthetic uppers and a soggy sole for $14.95 down the street, and your cheapest light touring shoe was a hand-lasted Norwegian jobbie with bull-hide uppers and a steel shank that sold for $35? Fortunately, the shops that specialize in ski touring did carry righteous gear, but even they were cautious about it. After all, the best shop in the universe does you no good if it goes out of business because the bulk of humanity goes down the street to the discount house.

The market's there now. Ski touring is such an appealing sport that the beginners who fell in love with it in droves weren't discouraged by shoddy, ill-fitting, fallapart boots. They simply upgraded their footgear, and as they outgrew the golf course, began looking for new horizons. Those new horizons necessitated a different kind of good boot. Now, thank heavens, old woodchucks like me can walk into my friendly local specialty shop and find three or four models of boots that are eminently suitable for backpacking on skis.

If all this seems remote from the problem of breaking trail on skis, it really isn't. The boot is one of the keys to enjoyable skiing with a heavy pack. Another key is the pack itself. If you plan to do a fair amount of backcountry skiing, do yourself a favor and buy a big internally-framed rucksack. The internally-framed rucksack rides closer to your body, snuggles in nearer to your center of gravity, and follows your movements better than a conventional packframe. The bottom line is that it's easier to ski with a big rucksack than with a packframe—particularly when you're beating your way through deep, soft snow, which provides a laterally unstable platform under your skis. Don't take my word for it. Go touring with a borrowed or rented internal-frame rucksack and see for yourself. I've used both in hard conditions; I wouldn't kid you. But you're not me. Possibly you'll be happier skiing with a frame. The only way you'll find out is to try both.

Proper boots and a pack that doesn't fight you will do you no harm, and will even help you a fair amount. But the biggest boost you'll get will come from simply paying attention to your skiing technique. I've been skiing—and teaching skiing—long enough to know that the backwoods skier may well harbor a lot of resentment against the "track skier." "Well, you come out with me someday with your skinny skis and your fancy bunny suit on and see what good your fancy kicking and gliding does you out here, fella. This is a man's world, and it isn't the place for you flashy resort bums." I get the same rap laid on me about my skinny racing canoes and bent-shaft paddles, too, but the skier is often more vehement about it and prouder of his ignorance, as it were. I'm not here to reform the world, believe me. But you'll run across these guys—they're *always* guys, by the way—if you do a lot of backwoods skiing. All I can do is prepare you for the shock—and hopefully teach you something.

There is a difference between skiing in untracked snow with a full pack and skiing on machine-set trails with ultralight gear. You'll find some difficulty in maintaining a fine, neutral position on soft snow with a pack on your back. It's harder to set your wax—or your waxless ski soles—in unconsolidated snow. Gliding in a foot of fresh snow isn't easy. But if you've been taught to ski in a neutral position, with a proper posture, you'll break trail easier because 1) you won't flail from side to side, 2) you'll depend on your legs and backside to move rather than your arms, and 3) you'll keep your movements centered around your center of gravity.

Getting your body "centered" is important. I have taught ski touring long enough to know that simple approaches are best. If you're skiing without a pack, your center of gravity is somewhere between your navel and your pubic bone. A pack raises that, of course, and moves it backwards, but don't worry about it. It doesn't matter. Right now, stand up and locate that spot with a finger. Press hard. Feel that spot inside you, cradled between your pelvic bones. Now, with your feet about 8 inches apart and your weight evenly distributed on them, move your body around that spot. Move your hips; move your torso; move your arms. Slowly, slowly—that's the way. Do an exaggerated, slow bump and grind; do what you think a belly dancer does. Slide your hips out to one side and then the other. As your mind relaxes, so will your body. You'll find yourself in positions that you used to consider un-balanced. But they're not, all of a sudden.

Now we'll do one more thing. You've skied; you know what it looks like when it's done right, even if you don't do it that way all the time. Put your right foot in front; imagine you're gliding on one ski. The knee is bent, of course, and your weight's evenly distributed on your foot. Now, swing your left leg back. Keep it pretty straight but not stiff. Use the muscles in the small of your back, your buttocks and your thighs to do it. *Feel* them work; be conscious of them. They're heavy, powerful muscles, and they're the ones that propel you. Use your arms for balance—left arm forward, right arm back, shoulders square to the imaginary track you're skiing on. Not bad—but if you're like most Americans, you'll keep your hips square to the track, particularly if you're a guy. Americans have been nurtured on the idea of an erect, military posture and a walk that uses no hip movement— which is a very inefficient and ultimately painful way to ski. Or to walk, for that matter. If you're squared away completely, you'll notice a lot of tension in that big set of muscles at the top of your thigh, beginning at the kneecap. Relax. Try it again, but this time think about pointing your right hip bone down the track. Not too much, now. Don't turn your body— just "lead" a little with your hip. Okay? Relax. Poke your belly with your finger and find your center, find your spot. Close your eyes and really nail its location down. Got it? Now go back and do this exercise again. Start it with your hip square and then slowly lead with the hip. Hmmm! Felt funny, didn't it? The magic spot felt like it dropped down inside your pelvic girdle as you led the hip a little, didn't it? Felt the tension in the thighs relaxed. Your stance is more secure and less fatiguing.

Don't ask why. Accept that it does, and enjoy it. And when you're in deep snow, or when you get a little tired and tense on the trail, find that magic spot and keep it nestled safely between your hip bones. Don't let it hang out in front of you or roll out over the back of the bowl formed by your hips.

You see, most people forget to *ski* when they put on a pack or get in deep snow. You can get away with sloppy, un- centered skiing on a track, because the conditions are so good. You shouldn't let this happen, regardless. Skiing is an end in itself—a remarkably lovely, fluid, poetically rhythmical set of body movements. When you tune your mind and body to the act of skiing, you'll find that your mind clears very quickly and you'll be seeing things like animal tracks and patterns of light and shade that you've never noticed. Your body's on automatic pilot, as it were—enjoying its own trip. Let your head enjoy *its* outing! Don't stop skiing. Keep centered, let those heavy, powerful, resilient muscles do their job of skating you forward. Don't get back on your heels and plod along, stomping the snow into submission. You don't have to ski that way in deep snow—if you can call it skiing.

Ski touring is hard, physical work. Skiing well is sweaty business in untracked snow—but so is snowshoeing, and so is skiing badly. You'll work up a sweat on skis, which means that your clothing has to be chosen even more carefully. I've worn crepe nylon knickers and a jersey for years, but a lot of folks are understandably leery about them and others are downright hostile. They're pretty—and meant to be pretty. Some of them border on the outlandish, I suppose. But the good quality ones do the job surpassingly well. If you can live with the price tag, and with the fact that some sour old woodchucks in Iron Boy pants will write you off as a resort skier, effeminate, or both, a good quality running suit of crepe nylon knickers and jersey is the way to fly.

I have several of these jobbies, but they're all of a type. They're all nylon, which both breathes and doesn't absorb moisture. The knickers are doubled across the belly, in the groin and down the front of the thighs. The jersey tops have collars that can be zipped into turtlenecks if necessary, and the fronts of the jerseys are doubled. The jerseys have zippered pockets in front—"kangaroo pockets"—and the knickers have a one zippered pocket. They're Norwegian-made. An Odlo, a Lifa, and one that bears a North Cape label and is probably a Janus. I've worn them in subzero weather, in 45° spring sun, in an all-day drizzle, and in cold, raw winds. I use the tops in chilly weather for canoe racing. Matter of fact, I've raced the 70-mile General Clinton marathon twice in one of these shirts, because it was warm enough to keep me cozy in chilly, drizzly early mornings and it breathed well enough to be bearable and then some in the heat of the day.

Of course you have to select your underwear (and outwear if necessary) to cope with different weather systems. The crepe nylon suits offer the skier a tremendously versatile garment that works in a wide range of temperature and humidity. They're worth the money. The cheap imitations—usually cotton and polyester "fluff"—aren't worth a nickel. You're better off by far to wear the traditional polyester/cotton hard-finished knickers and a jacket or shirt of whatever pleases you.

But do yourself a favor. Don't wear pants. Wear knickers. They're not a fashion item, for heaven's sake. Old Norwegian farmers wear them for skiing. Swedish grandmothers and Lapp herdsmen wear them for skiing. Why? Because they work, that's why. Your knees are free to flex without having to pull a chunk of fabric up tight across them. You don't have to tote around pounds of wet pantlegs and cuffs because there aren't any cuffs and there isn't much pantleg. And it's easier to change out your socks than it is to change out your pants! You can snip off some old woolen pants from your closet or the Salvation Army and make knickers out of them. Cut them longer in front than in the back—and cut them longer overall than you think you need—and close them with *Velcro* tabs, and presto! Lightweight wool or wool and synthetic knickers. Cheap! And good, too!

I could prattle for years about touring. I've taught it and helped develop a standard teaching method for it. But the more involved I get, the more I grow to feel that maybe we're institutionalizing it too much. We're growing too conscious of technical distinctions between skis that are so subtle that they don't transmit on the snow to anybody much below a world class skier. We've grown almost hidebound about instruction methods and about who is qualified to teach on a professional level. Now I'm not decrying progress. I've skied a lot of pairs of marvelous wooden skis in the past. Last year I spent most of my time on a pair of superlight fiberglass race training skis. As far as I'm concerned, my wooden skis have been virtually retired. The glass rockets are lighter, stronger, livelier and faster. Skiing a lot and skiing hard, I can sense the differences. If you're not interested in that kind of skiing, you don't need a fancy glass ski. And don't let anybody tell you otherwise! If you're turned on by the look of fine wood, ski wooden skis. Conversely, if you *like* to wax, use waxes. If you don't, ski a waxless ski. Just don't get so involved in the equipment and the subtle differences between Ski A and Ski B that you let it interfere with *skiing*.

Technique's a different matter. A sound, easy, fluid way of skiing is simply less work, and less work equates directly to more enjoyment as far as I'm concerned. But don't get so hung up on technique that you're skiing tensely, worrying about how you look. There's a fine line here. It's good to immerse yourself in what your body's doing. Listen to your body, feel the muscles work, enjoy the sensual delight of cradling your magic center spot in just the right place to make skiing easy. But until you can become immersed in the totality of it, forget the little picky points that the technicians love. Ski loose and easy, with a relaxed mind; when the time comes that you *want* to know how to do a double pole/kick maneuver, when the time comes that the bit of advanced technique looks like *fun* to you (and it is—it's sheer, exuberant **power!),** then you're ready to learn it. And when you're ready to learn, you'll learn so quickly that it slmost shocks you!

One more thing. Ski touring is preeminently a day tripper's pastime, although you can ski easily with a big pack in untracked snow and overnight as well if you choose. A sport that's almost inseparable in my mind with spring snow, sun, crusty Italian bread, salami, hard cheese and Mountain red, and *fun*. Make of it a "serious" sport if you wish. Lecture on the evils of wine in cold weather if you wish—and the evils of booze in cold weather are obvious—and tell me that I shouldn't go anywhere without a Nordic ski patrolman following in my footsteps. I'll concede all these things. And I'll even applaud your probity. But I'll continue to do it my way, thank you. And I hope you do the same. □

PACKS, PACKS, PACKS!

If you're a three-season walker—and I am'nt after callin' you a "hiker" because that's an *ugly* word—you already own a backpack of some sort (most probably a frame pack,) and a little daybag for short jaunts. I don't want to reinvent the wheel by giving you a long rap about packs. You own two of them, and common sense dictates that you make do with what you own already. After all, you're already in the barrel for things like a mountain parka, a supplemental sleeping bag, winter boots, a winter stove, snowshoes or touring skis and a host of other goodies. At this point, I assume that you'd rather not spend any more money. And you don't have to.

Not much, anyway. I'm a great fan of waterproof nylon covers for packs—either frame packs or big subframe rucksacks—because wet, clammy experience tells me that even waterproof nylon leaks. My own slovenly habits also necessitate a pack cover, I fear. I'm the guy who always fails to completely close two zippers. Having done this, wet snow or blizzard conditions inevitably (retributively??) arise and find these two partially open zippers. And what is inevitably within those two pockets? Spare mittens, toilet paper and pipe tobacco! So much for know-it-all magazine editors!

Most pack covers designed to fit frame packs will fit over the big internally-framed rucksacks that have become so popular of late. To be sure—and to be sure if you carry a frame pack as well—bring your pack to your friendly local outfitter's shop and try the cover on it.

Another thing that you might find useful for winter wandering is an extra pocket or two on your pack. Winter overnighting gear is likely heavier than summer gear—and it's certainly bulkier. You don't want your gear hanging off the pack if you can help it, and you may have trouble avoiding it by the time you've stuffed those bulky shirts and sweaters inside. Extra pockets are available. Kelty produces them for their pack line, so does Jan Sport. Needless to add, you don't *have* to match color and fabric. I backpacked for years with an ugly green Kelty pocket—one from the big BB5 packbag—on my ugly dirty orange Alp expedition bag, and while the purists may have been revolted by it, neither I nor the Canada jays minded a bit. And my down jacket had a cozy, accessible spot in which to travel.

Another thing you may want to do is attach some sort of thong or cord or dingbat to each zipper pull on the pack so you can open the pocket without fumbling or removing your mittens. I've used two-bit plastic tab keykeepers on my parka zippers for a couple of years now, and I'm thinking of putting them on the pack zippers in lieu of the cord now on them. Don't buy the things, for God's sake. Lots of businesses give them away as promos. In fact, if you're really stuck for one, drop me a note at *Wilderness Camping* (1597 Union St., Schenectady, N.Y. 12309) and I'll send you a genuine cheap plastic keytab with a metal ring on it for your parka or pack zipper. It'll say *Wilderness Camping* on it, of course—but then I'm sure you didn't expect me to send you one that read *Solemna Burial Gardens!*

All kidding aside, though, the pull cord or keychain dingbat is one of those deceptively simple modifications to your pack (and outer clothing) that makes your life so much simpler you'll wonder why you hadn't done it years before!

Another one of those "why didn't I do this years ago" things is sealing the seams of your pack—even if you have a separate raincover! Your outfitter has some sort of seam sealant made for coated nylon, most likely the stuff that Kenyon Mills packages. It's good. It should be. All that coated fabric you see around comes from Kenyon anyway, so can assume that their seam sealant will 1) work and 2) be compatible with the fabric and the coating. Seal the seams; that's where any waterproof fabric first leaks. And while you're fiddling around, you can also spray or brush a silicone water-repellent treatment on the zipper tapes. Zippers—even the molded Delrin ones—can freeze, and what makes them freeze is rarely ice in the teeth. It's a frozen zipper tape. Keep the tape dry and chances are good that the teeth will remain frost-free. I play this game with my pack zippers and my parka zippers as well, and I bub a little bit of paraffin on the teeth to boot. I've never had a zipper freeze up, either—and like Mark Twain and the toothache, I don't intend to have it happen in the future!

I've assumed that you already own a day bag and a frame pack. You may find that the bulky gear you carry in winter won't fit in the daybag. I'm not an equipment freak. What I've suggested that you carry represents something in the way of a minimum, so if that minimum for a long day trip doesn't fit in your daybag, you'll wind up taking your frame pack. As you know already, a frame pack isn't the greatest device for tight quarters or for those pastimes that require a degree of balance and movement, like ski touring and steep slope scrambling on snowshoes. You may want to consider purchasing a middle-sized rucksack like the old Alp Eiger for winter daytripping.

It's difficult to write intelligently about rucksacks unless I define size and use so narrowly that you have no real choices. I carry a huge Synergy Works subframe rucksack, an expedition bag if there ever was one, on family daytrips in hard country, on overnights, and on long long treks to the middle of nowhere and back again. This pack is admirably suited for all backpacking, winter and summer, but I must point out that any subframed rucksack of this class is an expensive piece of gear. If you find you like winter camping, and particularly if you plan to do a lot of it on skis, you'll wind up with a Synergy Works pack (or a Lowe or a Madden or a Hine-Snowbridge or a Karrimor or a Jan Sport or a Gerry or a Wilderness Experience or a Tough Traveler or any one of a dozen other big expedition bags, all of which are good).

Howsomever, that isn't the kind of pack we're talking about now. We're talking about the classic rucksack with two side pockets, a header pocket, well-padded shoulder straps, and a waistband to locate the load. This latter should tell you something. The big subframed packs, with massive padded hipbelts and internal frames that are either fastened directly to the hipbelt by some mechanical means or indirectly by a fabric link, are meant to carry heavy loads, and will transfer most of the load to your pelvic girdle. The smaller rucksacks, with waistbands rather than hipbelts, will *not* transfer any appreciable amount of load to your hips. It'll all hang from your shoulders. This means that you'll have to be watchful about how much weight you put into one. Twenty-five pounds is more than enough, even for a real moose of a guy—which I'm not. Look on the traditional rucksack as a *bulk* hauler rather than a *weight* hauler and you'll be much, much happier on the trail.

Some of these rucksacks—and they come in an appalling range of sizes and designs—are bespangled with pockets, straps, leather patches for more straps, and other goodies. Are these useful? To me, they are—but then the only time I use that kind of a pack is when I'm going in harm's way for a day, and need ice axe, crampons, and climbing snowshoes accessible at all times. Most of the time I carry my big sub-framed pack. If you like bells and whistles on a pack, get a pack with bells and whistles on it. It's that simple. I will enter one cautionary note, though. Load the rucksack at your out-fitter's, and check to see if you have good, free arm move-ment and head movement. You may be using this thing for skiing or for steep scrambling where mobility is all-important. Make sure that the pack you buy fits you comfortably—and if it doesn't, don't buy it. No number of "features" should ever outweigh fit in considering a pack. You'll be living with—or under—this thing for eight to ten hours a day in frequently difficult and sometimes enervating circumstances, and that pack has to fit you so well that you're barely conscious of its presence. The big subframed packs can, of course, be "tuned" to fit like a second skin through the expensive medium of adjusting tabs and straps. I can alter the functional width of my Synergy bag at the hips, the hipbelt position, the shoulder harness length and span, the yoke width of the harness, the tension of the mesh backband, the frame con-figuration, effective frame length and frame stiffness, and I can even alter the roll moment of the entire unit by moving pockets around or removing them altogether. This adap-tability, of course, comes at a price—$140, to be exact. The rucksack you're hunting for is nearer to $40, so you can't ex-pect a wide range of adjustments. It's imperative, therefore, to find one that *fits*, and then to load it within its—and your—design parameters.

You've heard this before, my friend, but I have to say it again because this is my last chance to say it. You're not going out there to prove anything. You're not going out there to rough it. You're going to smooth it. You get it rough enough every day! □

IN FROM THE COLD

When I finished *Movin' Out* in the autumn of 1974, I couldn't resist closing it with a quotation from Mark Twain's *Huckleberry Finn:*

"*...And so there ain't nothing more to write about, and I am rotten glad of it, because if I'd a knowed what a trouble it was to make a book I wouldn't a tackled it and ain't agoing to no more. But I reckon I got to light out for the Territory ahead of the rest, because Aunt Sally she's going to adopt me and sivilize me and I can't stand it. I been there before.*"

Well, I knowed already what a trouble it was to make a book, and I came back and made another one—which means, I suppose, that my learning curve is a lot flatter than Huck's.

But I haven't been civilized yet, and maybe it's because I light out for the Territory every chance I get. Granted, the Territory usually is the hill behind our farmhouse, but it's the Territory for sure as long as my head's buttoned on straight.

And may you always have some Territory to light out for, my friend, before somebody civilizes you.

Like Huck, we've all been there before. □